living organized

living organized

proven steps for a clutter-free
and beautiful home

sandra felton

Revell
Grand Rapids, Michigan

Published by Fleming H. Revell
a division of Baker Publishing Group
P.O. Box 6287, Grand Rapids, MI 49516-6287
www.bakerbooks.com

Revised edition of *The Messies Superguide*

Printed in the United States of America

Library of Congress Cataloging-in-Publication Data
Felton, Sandra.
    Living organized : proven steps for a clutter-free and beautiful
home / Sandra Felton.
        p.   cm.
    Rev. ed. of : Messies superguide. c1987
    Includes bibliographical references.
    ISBN 0-8007-5945-1 (pbk.)
    1. House cleaning. I. Felton, Sandra. Messies superguide. II. Title.
TX324.F43497 2004
648′.5—dc22   2004004546

Unless otherwise indicated, Scripture is taken from the King James Version of the Bible.

Scripture marked NIV is taken from the HOLY BIBLE, NEW INTERNA-TIONAL VERSION®. NIV®. Copyright © 1973, 1978, 1984 by International Bible Society. Used by permission of Zondervan. All rights reserved.

The "Won't-Pick-Up-Toys Cure" on pages 35–44 is taken from chapter 2 (pp. 23–26) of *Mrs. Piggle-Wiggle* by Betty MacDonald (J. B. Lippincott). Text copyright 1947 by Betty MacDonald. Renewed 1975 by Donald C. MacDonald. Reprinted by permission of Harper & Row, Publishers, Inc.

"The MAGIC ROOM" on page 167 is a proprietary service mark belonging to Rebecca Emerick and is used only with her expressed permission.

The chart on pages 24–25 is taken from *Drawing on the Right Side of the Brain* by Betty Edwards, copyright © 1979 by Betty Edwards, published by Jeremy P. Tarcher, Inc. It is used by permission of St. Martin's Press, Inc.

Contents

Acknowledgments

Most authors acknowledge more people in their acknowledgments than I know now or have ever known in my life. A lot of the people they mention are really big names, too. It leaves me somewhat embarrassed that I don't have a long list to mention here. Perhaps, however, that fact will serve to highlight those who helped in their own way in their contribution to this book. Thanks go to the people following:

First, to Dr. Wendy Cheyney, whom I found in a miraculously wonderful way. I was walking by the center fountain at the park-like Florida International University campus on a sparkling day wondering where inside those mammoth buildings I might find help in my research. So clearly came the memory of the verse, "seek, and ye shall find" (Matt. 7:7). I went to the Psychology Department, but everyone was busy or out. I went to the Education Department, and Dr. Cheyney was "in" on unscheduled office hours and had a rare nonbusy moment. She was invaluable in talking to me about brain research. She and I both believe our meeting was not mere happenstance.

Second, to Barbara Taggert, who along with her husband, Bill, in the Business Department at Florida International University have done much study in the application of brain research to business management. Their work contributed much to this book.

When last Barbara was in England holding a seminar, she spoke with Prince Charles about their brain research findings and told me if ever it came up she would mention Messies Anonymous to the queen. I mention the queen only because I want to use all the big names I possibly can.

Third, to all the folks at Fleming Revell who have continued confidence in the Messies Anonymous principles.

Fourth, to Tina, as always, who has worked with me almost from the beginning of M.A. and is superimportant in many ways, and to Harriet, who in her quiet, happy way, helps take up the slack so I can do my part.

Fifth, a very special acknowledgment to Rebecca Emerick, an upbeat, talented interior decorator who understands the Messie problem from the inside and contributed the three chapters on decorating.

Do You Need This Book?

If your answer to the above question is a resounding "Yes!" you might as well skip this page and get right into high gear. If you're not sure, taking this little quiz may confirm what you've suspected all along but haven't had the nerve to admit—you are a card-carrying Messie.

1. When I last had an appointment with my doctor, I
   a. arrived ten minutes early so I could enjoy leafing through the newest *National Geographic*.
   b. arrived just as the patient before me was coming out of the examination room.
   c. never arrived because I couldn't find the car keys.

2. The thing that most frightens my children is
   a. the thought of being killed in a car accident.
   b. the threat of international chaos.

c. the possibility that one of their friends might come to our house without giving a two-week warning.

3. The last time I cleaned the oven was
   a. just yesterday after I finished baking six dozen homemade sugar cookies for the church bazaar.
   b. about three weeks ago—I always clean the oven at the end of each month.
   c. eight years ago, after we put out the grease fire in the boiler.

4. The books in our house are
   a. neatly arranged by topic on floor-to-ceiling shelves in the den.
   b. beginning to fill our available storage space.
   c. holding up one end of the coffee table.

5. For me, cleaning out closets is
   a. a rarity since my closets seldom require cleaning.
   b. a good morning's work but worth the effort.
   c. on a par with having a root canal.

6. At my house, we save
   a. nothing—it only leads to clutter.
   b. aluminum cans which we then take to the recycling center regularly.
   c. old *TV Guides*.

7. . . . and we collect
   a. antique Chinese porcelain plates.
   b. trading stamps.
   c. dust.

8. We sometimes use paper plates at our house because
   a we enjoy barbecuing out on the patio.
   b. they're helpful when everyone's in a hurry.
   c. there are no clean dishes left.

9. When we have guests, I
   a. always take them on a complete tour of our home.
   b. try to keep them out of the basement— it's a little cluttered.
   c. padlock the bedroom doors.

10. When we visit other people's homes, I
   a. enjoy seeing how their décor reflects their personalities.
   b. look for a cobweb or two so I know they're not perfect.
   c. write the wrong address in the guest book in case they ever decide to visit us.

Straight *C*s? Read on, fellow Messies. There's help . . . and hope.

Introduction

How to Read This Book

Read this book with a pen in your hand and one of those yellow or pink highlighters beside you if you can find one and keep up with it. As you read, feel free to write in the margins thoughts, feelings, and examples as they occur to you. Underline and write *NB* beside significant parts. (*NB* for the Latin words *Nota Bene* or "observe well" or "look carefully." I first saw it in a book owned by Norma Banas and thought she was writing her initials in the margins.)

There are spots in this book to fill in answers and ideas. Try to complete the exercises in each section. If you skip over any without filling them in, that's perfectly okay. Just keep going on without worrying about it. But they are easy to answer and will be very fulfilling for you if you do them.

As you read, turn down page corners to mark sections that are important to you. You will want to look back from time to time. Write a word or two on the flap you turned down. Use a bookmark or (who can keep track of an official bookmark?) a corner torn off the morning newspaper to mark your place so you won't get confused by extra folded-down corners. If you have sticky notes, use those to keep your place and as tab reminders for important things.

Try not to lose the book while you are reading it because, if you do, you'll lose your enthusiasm for the insights you get. Here is your first fill-in for where you will faithfully store the book:

I will keep this book _____ while I am reading it.

You may also want to choose, with some care, when and where you read this. If you are not at home when your enthusiasm begins to bubble, you may find yourself under a lot of stress because you can't start on the house right away.

You see, this really is your kind of book. Use it well.

part 1

Cleaning
with the Right Side
of Your Brain

1

It's All in Your Mind

The Right-Brained Messie

Why are all of us in the world so different from one another? Why was my brother a Cleanie and I a Messie? Why do we have disorganized and laid-back people and also precise, systematically organized people? Is it heredity? Is it training?

In the early 1960s, a medical discovery was made that will help us to understand why we function so differently. A forty-two-year-old man, referred to in medical literature as W. J., sought help for very severe epileptic seizures brought on by an injury suffered in World War II.

No amount of medication could control his seizures. They would begin on one side of the brain and cross the corpus callosum (a bundle of nerves that connects the two hemispheres of the brain) to the other side. The doctors surmised that if they cut the corpus callosum—the bridge, so to speak—the seizures would be confined to one side and they could control this smaller area with medication. That, to their delight, was exactly what happened. Later, the surgery was performed on a total of twelve people. All of these patients returned quickly to normal functioning without any apparent effects of having the right side of the brain severed from communication with the left side. Subsequent testing showed this was far from true.

Without going into details about the experiments, here is what they learned:

The left and right sides of the brain do not function as mirror images of each other in the way our lungs and kidneys do. In fact, they are quite different. Researchers have discovered that each side of the brain has its own area of specialization. Each hemisphere has its own "way of knowing" and processes information differently. In a normal brain, the two sides work together by means of the corpus callosum, that four-inch, pencil-shaped bundle of nerves cut in the patients who had epilepsy. Even though we use both sides of our brain, some of us are left-brain dominant and some of us are right-brain dominant.

The left brain is verbal, logical, and analytical.

The left brain specializes in all those areas that help people fit into the way our society—and especially our school system—is structured today. The left brain is verbal, logical, and analytical. It puts things in order, lines them up, counts them, and makes step-by-step plans. The left side of the brain controls the right side of the body. To remember what the left brain does, imagine a bold, block **L**—straight, orderly, and no-nonsense.

The right brain, which controls the left side of the body, is intuitive and sees things spatially—that is, how parts relate to one another and fit together to form a whole. It understands metaphors, doesn't require reason or facts to make judgments, and lacks a sense of time. It is creative and doesn't require words to understand or express concepts. The right brain is not good at sequencing (doing one thing first, then the next, then the next) or putting things into categories. To help you remember what the right brain does, think of a curvy, complex, fanciful capital *R*.

If you're beginning to see Cleanies and Messies lurking behind these left-brain/right-brain pictures, you may be on to something. Perhaps as you were reading these descriptions of the two brains you immediately thought of people you know—creative, artistic, daydreamer types (right-brain dominant) or friends who are punctual, organized, A students (left-brain dominant). Maybe you saw yourself in one of these descriptions.

> The right brain is not good at sequencing . . . or putting things into categories.

Knowing a little about *how* we think is an important preliminary to learning how to make our thinking work for us, not against us. Stop for a minute and think about yourself. Chances are that if you're reading this book you are a Messie and by now you must have figured out that Messies are generally right-brain-dominant people. We're the freewheeling folk who often have trouble fitting into a straight-laced world. We just weren't made to arrange the spice rack alphabetically, yet we do have to conform to a point so that our houses are not health and fire hazards, our children are fed and clothed, and we aren't fired from our jobs for perpetual tardiness.

Being right-brain dominant is certainly not a curse—many people would give their cross-referenced photo albums for a little of the uninhibited creativity that comes naturally to us. We Messies need to understand that what we lack are coping skills, ways to harness our thinking styles into systems and patterns and habits that will help us live more joyful, hassle-free lives.

In the rest of this chapter, we'll dig a little deeper into how our brains work, how all this "brain business" shows up in our lifestyles, and just what we ought to do about it.

While many of us are characterized by which side of our brain is dominant, we do most of our day-to-day, garden-variety thinking using both of the brain's hemispheres. Have you ever said about someone, "I can't put my finger on it, but there's something about him that bothers me"? or read all the literature about your candidates, made your choices, and, once you were in the voting booth, picked candidates based on how you felt? Maybe you've heard of someone who had no luck at all coming up with a solution to a complex problem and then dreamed the answer.

> "There is occasions and causes why and wherefore in all things."
>
> —William Shakespeare

All of these are examples of the two sides of our brain cooperating together to process and understand information. The analytical left brain looks at everything logically and in order; then the intuitive right brain jumps in with a burst of insight, and all of a sudden the pieces fit together. Remember the story about Archimedes in his bathtub? After toiling over some sticky math problems (having to do with water displacement), he stopped for a long, hot soak, giving his left brain enough time off so that his right brain could help him put what he knew into the right order. "Eureka!" he is said to have cried as he discovered his solution and gave California a state motto all at the same time.

Decision making is a problem for Messies, and it's one where both sides of our brain need to work together. We let the left brain look at the pros and cons, analyze all the related information, and make sure the facts are straight. Then we check with the right brain to see if the decision feels right. This is called the mixed approach. It is an effective way to make decisions. The person's dominant side acts as the "umpire," the final arbiter, which uses the nondominant side for input.

Sometimes we feel paralyzed when trying to make a decision. This is the integrated approach—information comes from too many sources and has no "umpire" to tell it which way to go. I suspect this may be the problem with some perfectionistic Messies. They want to do everything exactly right and fear making any decision they may regret later. So much information bombards the perfectionist Messie's mind that both the right and left sides of the brain get overloaded and the whole thing begins to short out. "I feel paralyzed," said Grace, a self-confessed Messie as she described her struggle with perfectionism.

> Decision making is a problem for Messies, and it's one where both sides of our brain need to work together.

Example of the Purple Blouse Dilemma

L-Left (Logical Side)	R-Right (Intuitive Side)
I ought to get rid of this purple blouse. I haven't worn it in two years and probably won't wear it again.	But purple is coming back into style.
It takes up room in the closet. I would be better off without it.	But I paid a lot of money for it and haven't worn it much. And it still has all the buttons.
I hate purple. I know I won't ever wear it.	Perhaps I'll learn to love purple. People do change, you know. Then I'll wish I had it.
It's foolish to keep something you don't want.	It might look nice with my white skirt that's at the cleaners.

Back and forth it goes with logic pulling one way and feeling another until the poor brain fizzles out and gives up. The blouse stays in the closet not because the brain decided to keep it but because the brain decided not to decide.

One area related to decision making where right-brain dominance can show up is the *desire to avoid frustration*. Strangely enough, Cleanies have the same desire but go about achieving it differently.

The Messie who comes home and takes off her shoes in the living room may not wish to take them to the bedroom closet because that additional bit of work is an annoyance. It is more pleasing to flop down in a chair and watch TV instead. She promises herself she'll take the shoes (and the books and folded laundry) to the bedroom the next time she goes there. Because it is characteristic for the Messie to not be in tune visually, it doesn't bother her that this stuff is lying around out of place. When the time comes for her to put on her shoes, she can't find them—at least not without a lot of searching. She is in a hurry and now she has *super* frustration. "Has anybody seen my black shoe? It was right here with this one!" She is really annoyed. Yet this is the same person who desperately wanted to avoid frustration when she didn't put away her shoes to begin with. People who let things go now pay for it later, or, as Ben Franklin might have said, a (frustrating) stitch in time now saves nine (frustrating) stitches later.

The right-brained Cleanie also has a low tolerance for frustration and avoids it like the plague. Dog-tired from work, the hungry Cleanie will hang up every piece of clothing and put the shoes on the shoe rack before resting or eating.

A woman on a call-in radio program in Chicago told me of her Cleanie husband who, when he comes home from a party where he has had too much to drink, weaves around until he gets his clothes hung up and even threads his two socks into the round plastic holder he uses to keep them together in the wash. No matter how difficult, he keeps on until he succeeds.

Why do Cleanies sometimes insist on such rigorous behavior from themselves? They don't like to see things out of place, but, more importantly, they desperately want to avoid the frustration of not knowing where something is. They work hard now to avoid problems later on. Mess up a Cleanie's hard-won order, and you will feel the heat of that frustration.

Cleanies can be obnoxious, annoying, and extreme, but they can also have guests over at the drop of a hat. They can surround themselves with beauty and leave the house without feeling guilty. The energy they put into avoiding frustration is worth the sense of order and well-being. The Messie method of avoiding frustration by leaving things undone saps energy and only defers frustration.

> "Intelligence is the quickness in seeing things as they are."
>
> —George Santayana

Let's review. Rapid, effective decision making is necessary for keeping things in order. The integrated approach is hard. The Messie who wears herself out with perfectionist overload will not be able to make the decisions necessary to run her life. The Messie who constantly decides to put off the frustration of immediate effort will find herself in a seriously disorganized house with a big mess on her hands. The only way out of the forest is to change this approach to thinking.

1. If you could make decisions more easily, would you be less messy? Explain.

2. Are you such a perfectionist that you find it hard to make a decision or carry it out? Explain and give an example.

3. Do you feel that you put things off in order to avoid frustration? Give an example.

4. What change in your thinking might you consider in order to make decisions easier?

5. What was the most significant insight you found in this chapter, and how can you put it to use?

A Comparison of Left-Mode and Right-Mode Characteristics

L-Mode	R-Mode
Verbal: using words to name, describe, define.	*Nonverbal:* Awareness of things, but minimal connection with words.
Analytic: Figuring things out step-by-step and part-by-part.	*Synthetic:* Putting things together to form wholes.
Symbolic: Using a symbol to stand for something. For example, the drawn form 👁 stands for eye; the sign + stands for the process of addition.	*Concrete:* Relating to things as they are, at the present moment.
Abstract: Taking out a small bit of information and using it to represent the whole thing.	*Analogic:* Seeing likenesses between things; understanding metaphoric relationships.
Temporal: Keeping track of time, sequencing one thing after another: doing first things first, second things second, etc.	*Nontemporal:* Without a sense of time.
Rational: Drawing conclusions based on reason and facts.	*Nonrational:* Not requiring a basis of reason or facts; willingness to suspend judgment.
Digital: Using numbers as in counting.	*Spatial:* Seeing where things are in relation to other things and how parts go together to form a whole.
Logical: Drawing conclusions based on logic: one thing following another in logical order; for example, a mathematical theorem or a well-stated argument.	*Intuitive:* Making leaps of insight, often based on incomplete patterns, hunches, feelings, or visual images.

Linear: Thinking in terms of linked ideas, one thought directly following another, often leading to a convergent conclusion.	*Holistic:* Seeing whole things all at once; perceiving the overall patterns and structures, often leading to divergent conclusions.

Thank you for your book, "The Messies Manual." It has become a major force in my home. (I would handwrite this, but excited handwriting is hard to read.) When I first bought it, my husband thought it was just one more way to procrastinate as I am an avid reader and sat down immediately to read it cover to cover.

I can't begin to tell you what it meant to me. I laughed, cried, and got a "high" that lasted for days. It even gave me a lift at work where I've felt burnt-out for years. The first thing I did was Mt. Vernonize my kitchen on my day off—actually took two days, but what a world of difference. Now my husband is almost ready to lead the way into the next room—the living room. He hasn't read the book, but admits the kitchen is a vast improvement. (I think he has doubts that it will remain this way, though.)

The lone passage that made me a believer in you and your book was the reference you made to a study on how one knows their left from their right. I'm 33 and have never known! I have to look at my wedding ring and remember that it is on my left hand! It was a real problem before I was married! Even knowing I write with my right doesn't help. When in the car, directions have to be given as "turn your way" or "turn my way." I'm sure many people thought that was a joke, though I have always admitted I couldn't tell right from left. I cried with relief to realize I'm not alone. (Immediately on reading that passage to my husband, he assumed that that was going to be my next excuse.)

Thank you for the order you have already given to my life and home.

Barb / Michigan

2

Messies, Creativity, and the Inner Child

I was amazed as I read the accounts of creative people in Marilee Zdenek's book *The Right Brain Experience* (McGraw-Hill) to see two patterns begin to emerge.

Child-Oriented

Creative Messies are very childhood-oriented. They are quite comfortable with the "child" in themselves and don't try to hide it or bury it under the adult logic of the left brain.

Obviously, Charles Schulz, the inventor of the *Peanuts* comic strip, was child-oriented. Charlie Brown represents the child in Charles Schultz. Although he lost most of his childhood belongings in a fire, Schulz highly valued one drawing a teacher saved and sent to him many years later. He reported, "I used to think of that drawing all the time—and then I opened up an envelope one day and there it was."

Charles Schulz drew heavily on the associations of colors; the purple of a Porsche reminded him of a top he had at age twelve; a certain copper color reminded him of the jacks he played with at school.

Entertainer Steve Allen did not keep things from his own childhood, but when he became an adult, he put value on preserving the childhood of his own four sons. "I saved every piece of paper that they produced from the time they were babies and now none of them would take a million dollars for that collection."

Writer Ray Bradbury, author of *Dandelion Wine* and the screenplay for *Moby Dick,* has filled his basement with books and toys dating from when he was three years of age. He calls his office a nest where he is surrounded with the "images of all the things I love."

Robert McKim, professor of a creative course called Visual Thinking at Stanford University, keeps in his home office his teddy bear and a picture of his grammar school class. He has things from his father's childhood as well, just to keep himself in touch with the creative child within him.

Interestingly enough, a few days before I began this book, I cleaned out my closet (again), peeling another layer off the onion of belongings. From the closet shelf, I retrieved my teddy bear, who had been waiting there for twenty years, wrapped in a plastic bag that was in shreds. My eighteen-year-old son had never seen it, although the two had shared the same house all those years. As I write, Teddy sits watching. "I'm glad you're back, Teddy. You've been away too long."

Keeping one's childhood vibrant by using memories and memorabilia from childhood is apparently a technique used by many right-brained, creative people. They do it subconsciously because they value the creative impulses of the child part of their adult lives. Adults who wish to be creative do well to keep that fun-loving, impulsive, visionary part of their natures alive so that it won't get pressured out of existence by the duties of grown-up lives.

This is what makes Messies such wonderful people. We are (as a group, not always as individuals) creative, imaginative, fun-loving, idealistic, visionary, and sentimental.

These are all qualities right-brained people admire. However, in the same package with the good childlike qualities we encourage in ourselves, there are other not-so-admirable qualities. These cause us problems. In order to control them, we must recognize them for what they are.

Desire for instant gratification. Why do I not put back the mayonnaise jar before I eat my sandwich? Because I want that sandwich immediately. I can't wait.

Why do I drop my purchases by the front door? Because I want to rest now. I can't wait.

Distractibility. Messies have a hard time confining their attention to one thing. Sometimes we leave things half done or undone simply because we have difficulty keeping to the job. We may leave our groceries in the bags on the kitchen counter, not primarily because we are exhausted, but because we've had enough of the grocery task and are ready to do something new. We have been grocery shopping for over an hour. We become impatient to switch away from groceries, and so we begin to fold clothes or read the mail. We tell ourselves that we are just too busy to put the groceries away right now. Cleanies would have put them away. Why don't we? Our attention span has reached its limit.

Low tolerance for hurt. Somehow Messies have a hard time coming to the realization that some jobs we must do are unpleasant and tiring. It is difficult for us

29

to accept that giving away "stuff" will hurt us, but that it is okay to be hurt. Optimistically, like children, we feel that if a job is hard, we really can't be expected to do it.

Lack of control of our lives. Children do not take control of the decisions and activities of their lives. In a strange way, many of us who are dynamic, responsible, successful people in the business world relinquish the control of our things and our time in our own homes.

We do not take control over throwing things out, feeling that "life" will take care of them. Perhaps we feel they will come and go as life ebbs and flows. Experience shows that life is not a careful housekeeper.

> "You owe it to all of us to get on with what you're good at."
>
> —W. H. Auden

We frequently do not plan out our time schedule, preferring to leave ourselves open for whatever "life" sends our way that day.

We are optimistically dependent on the goodwill and help of others in a sort of random way. We start out feeling confident that life is good and wise, and we will not try to thwart its natural workings by taking control.

In a very real way, we are taught this by some children's stories. Cinderella was helpless in the face of circumstances. She tried to work things out herself, but she finally gave up, defeated. However, a force outside herself came along in the form of the Fairy Godmother. Without any effort on her part, Cinderella became beautiful and was given a coach to get to the ball.

Moral: We can try to work things out, but it will be ineffective. Outside powerful forces will help us reach our goals.

Little Red Riding Hood tried to do good but got in serious trouble. Only an outside force, the woodsman, brought her help.

30

Moral: We are helpless, but there is a powerful force outside the door to rescue us just in time.

In both of these cases, real help came when the worker was most passive. I don't know about you, but I do know that I wasted a lot of time subconsciously waiting for "life" to rescue me—and it never did. I got as passive as I could about taking control of my things and my time but no woodsman rushed in. No godmother waved her wand. It was a jolt to realize they were never going to come—in fact did not even exist. *I* was the only godmother or woodsman I would ever see—I had to rescue myself.

> Childhood dreams die hard, but from their grave rises up a stronger force.

Childhood dreams die hard, but from their grave rises up a stronger force, a real force—the power we can all exercise over our own lives.

Interestingly enough, other stories read to children are designed to teach that we need to strive ourselves to accomplish our goals.

The Little Engine That Could purred its way to success. The third little pig showed us that only by hard work can we save ourselves from the wolf outside the door. The story of the grasshopper who played all summer and the ants who worked preparing for the winter showed us that we must think and plan ahead to care for ourselves or we will be in big trouble.

Possession-Oriented

Not only are creative right-brained people childhood-oriented, some are also possession-oriented. Charles Schulz saved his cartoons, of course. Steven Allen had sixteen hundred black three-ring loose-leaf notebooks full of his ideas at his house, saved to give to a university.

31

For some reason, Messies (and not all of the people we've mentioned are necessarily Messies—they may have their "saving" under control) tie themselves very strongly to their possessions, especially the possessions that relate to their childhood or their children or ideas they value. It also seems that Messies keep childhood items around to stimulate the creative child within them. Messies may feel exhaustion, fright, or despair when they "let go" of something saved because they are losing supervision of an important part of themselves.

> "Compared to what we ought to be and can be, we are only half awake."
>
> —William James

Let's look at our attitude in a slightly different way. Messies tend to feel that their possessions are "alive." We know that children feel this way about their dolls and stuffed animals. Adults, too, sometimes give life-like qualities to inanimate objects. In the heat of a golf tournament, people in the gallery yell at a ball that is about to miss the hole, "Turn, turn!" Some people give lifelike qualities to their cars, calling them by name and talking to them. The Pet Rock craze was an amazing example of people lightheartedly being willing to give inanimate objects the quality of life. Messies may do this to a greater degree than most.

Messies who have trouble letting go of their things sometimes feel they have a responsibility to see that their possessions get a good home if indeed they are willing to let them out on their own at all. A man I knew gave away a set of lacquered trays to a friend he felt would value them. However, when he saw the trays at the friend's house, they were not in a prominent place and were in an area he felt was too dry for the trays. He told me he had learned his lesson—not to give away his things again.

32

The truth is that right-brained people are uniquely wonderful. We add verve and magic to the workaday world around us. The truth also is that without realizing it, we have retained some ways of thinking that we must challenge. Otherwise we hurt those wonderful right-brained people—ourselves.

We need to clear out the cluttered way of thinking that makes us feel that, somehow, someone is going to rescue us from our unproductive way of functioning in regard to the housework. Then we will be free to move in our own behalf.

> The truth is that right-brained people are uniquely wonderful.

We need to clear out the cluttered way of thinking that makes us keep a vast number of belongings so that those belongings which truly are important to us get lost in the shuffle.

We've covered a lot of ground in this chapter. Maybe you've learned something important about yourself or people you know and love. Maybe you've discovered places in your life that need some renovating. Maybe you've just garnered a few interesting bits of information to pass along at the next party you attend. At any rate, we still have a way to go in this book. Everything else you read in *Living Organized* will relate to what you've already read. Hold on tight to that pink highlighter so you can mark the areas that deal with organizational problems you're having. Look for the Super Solutions and the Time Savers and an old friend, the Mount Vernon Method. And remember, I did promise you some coping skills a few pages ago. They're in here too, so read on.

1. Do you feel that you are creative? If so, in what ways?

2. Write about a childhood memory that is important to you. (It doesn't necessarily have to be related to messiness, but that would be good.)

3. What was your favorite childhood story? What about it appealed to you?

4. Do you ever feel "motherly" toward your possessions? Explain.

5. Do you keep reminders of childhood (such as possessions and pictures) around you? If so, which ones?

6. Write about the first time you realized you were less organized than others.

7. Write a short history of messiness in your life.

8. What is there about your possessions that makes them important to you?

9. Do you have any ways of thinking that you feel may keep you from taking control of your house and your life?

10. What ways of productive thinking have occurred to you as a result of reading this chapter?

Mrs. Piggle Wiggle
and the Won't-Pick-Up-Toys Cure

Hubert was a very lucky little boy whose grand-father always sent him wonderful toys for Christmas. Hubert's mother said that his grandfather sent him these marvelous presents because Hubert was such a dear little boy. His father said that it was to make up for that awful name they had wished on him. Hubert was named for his grandfather. His full name was Hubert Egbert Prentiss.

Hubert liked the presents his grandfather sent him, but who wouldn't? He had an electric train with track that went four times around his bedroom and into the closet and out again and had seven stations and every signal there was and two bridges and a snow shed. He also had a Little-Builder set so large that he could build regular office buildings; and a great big wagon full of stone blocks made into shapes so that he could build big stone bridges for his electric train and stone build-ings and even stone barracks for his one thousand and five hundred toy soldiers. Hubert also had a circus with every kind of wooden, jointed animal and clowns and tightrope walkers and trapeze artists. He had a little typewriter, and a real desk and a little radio and two automobiles. He had about a hundred or more airplanes and little cars. He had a fire engine with real sirens and lights and hook and ladders; and so many books that he had to have two book cases in his room.

Hubert liked all of his toys and he was moderately generous about letting other children play with them, but he never put his things away. When his mother made his bed she had to pick her way around and in and out and over the electric train and track. She had to take circus performers off the bureau and the bedposts. She had to pick up books that had been thrown face down on the floor and she was continually gathering up the Little-Builder set. It used to take her about three hours to do Hubert's room and about one hour to do the rest of her housework.

She would send Hubert up to put his toys away, but all he ever did was to stuff them under the bed or into the closet and in the morning when his mother cleaned his room, there they were for her to pick up.

Mrs. Prentiss was getting a little bored with this.

One rainy Saturday Hubert invited all of his little friends to play up in his room. He had Dicky and Charlie and Billy and Tommy and Bobby. They got out every single toy that Hubert owned and played with them and then, just before dinner, they all went home and left the mess. Hubert's mother didn't know a thing about this until the next morning when she went in to make Hubert's bed. Then she just stood in the doorway and looked. The electric train track went under the bed five times and under the bureau and under the chairs and around the desk and into the closet. All along the track were bridges and buildings of the stone blocks and whole towns built from the Little-Builder set. On the bed and under the bed and on the bureau were the circus tent, the animals, the clowns, the tightrope walkers and the

36

trapeze artists. The floor was littered with books and little automobiles and airplanes and painting sets and chemical sets and woodburning sets and crayons and coloring books and the little typewriter and the printing set and teddy bears and balls and jacks and Parcheesi games and jigsaw puzzles and soldiers, soldiers, soldiers.

She took two aspirin tablets and then telephoned her friend, Mrs. Bags. She said, "Hello, Mrs. Bags, this is Hubert's mother and I am so disappointed in Hubert. He has such lovely toys—his grandfather sends them to him every Christmas, you know—but he does not take care of them at all. He just leaves them all over his room for me to pick up every morning."

Mrs. Bags said, "Well, I'm sorry, Mrs. Prentiss, but I can't help you because you see, I think it is too late."

"Why, it's only nine-thirty," said Hubert's mother. "Oh, I mean late in life," said Mrs. Bags. "You see, we started Ermintrude picking up her toys when she was six months old. 'A place for everything and everything in its place,' we have always told Ermintrude. Now, she is so neat that she becomes hysterical if she sees a crumb on the floor."

"Well, I certainly hope she never sees Hubert's room," said Mrs. Prentiss dryly. "She'd probably have a fit." And she hung up the phone.

Then she called Mrs. Moohead. "Good Morning, Mrs. Moohead," she said. "Does Gregory pick up his toys?"

"Well, no he doesn't," said Mrs. Moohead. "But you know Gregory is rather delicate and I feel that just playing with his toys tires him so much that I personally see that all of his little friends put the toys away before they go home."

"That is a splendid idea," said Hubert's mother, "but I am trying to train Hubert, not his playmates."

"Well, of course, Hubert is very strong and healthy, but Gregory is intelligent," said Mrs. Moohead.

"Is he?" said Mrs. Prentiss crossly, because she resented this inference that her son was all brawn and no brain.

"Oh, dear," squealed Mrs. Moohead, "I think Gregory is running a temperature. I must go to him." She hung up the phone.

Mrs. Prentiss then called Mrs. Grapple. "Hello, Marge," she said. "How's Susan?"

Mrs. Grapple said, "I've punished her seven times since breakfast and I just heard a crash so she is probably getting ready for another. How's Hubert?"

"That's what I called about," said Mrs. Prentiss. "Can you suggest a way to make Hubert *want* to pick up his toys? His room looks like a toy store after an earthquake."

"Why don't you call this Mrs. Piggle-Wiggle? I have heard she is perfectly wonderful. All the children in town adore her and she has a cure for everything. As soon as I spank Susan, I'm going to call her."

Hubert's mother said, "Thank you very much, Marge. That is just what I'll do. I had forgotten about Mrs. Piggle-Wiggle, but I just know she can help me."

So she called Mrs. Piggle-Wiggle and said, "Mrs. Piggle-Wiggle, I hate to bother you, but you seem always to know what to do about children and I'll confess that I don't know what to do to make Hubert put his toys away."

Mrs. Piggle-Wiggle said, "Hubert is the sweet little boy with all the wonderful toys that his grandfather sends him, isn't he?"

Mrs. Prentiss said, "Why, yes, but I didn't know that you knew him."

"Oh, yes," said Mrs. Piggle-Wiggle. "Hubert and I are old friends. In fact, he is building an automobile in my back yard out of orange crates and empty tomato cans. Hubert is a very good carpenter."

Hubert's mother thought of the two little automobiles with rubber tires, real horns, leather seats big enough for two boys and lights that turned on with a switch, that Hubert's grandfather had given him; and she wondered why in the world he would want to build an automobile out of old orange crates and tomato cans. She said, however, "So that is where he and Dicky go every afternoon. I certainly hope he behaves himself."

"Oh, he does," said Mrs. Piggle-Wiggle. "We are all very fond of Hubert. But this problem of his toys. Let me see." Mrs. Piggle-Wiggle was quiet for some time. Then she said, "I think that the best thing for you to use is my old-fashioned Won't-Pick-Up-Toys cure. Starting now, don't pick up any of Hubert's toys. Don't make his bed. In fact, do not go into his room. When his room becomes so messy he can't get out of it, call me." Mrs. Piggle-Wiggle said goodbye and hung up the phone.

Hubert's mother, looking very relieved, went gaily about her housework, baked a chocolate cake for dinner and did not say a word to Hubert when he came home with ten little boys and they all trailed upstairs to play in Hubert's room.

The next morning when Hubert came downstairs for breakfast his mother noticed that he had a little pan of water-color paint stuck in his hair and his shirt had purple ink from the printing set on one shoulder. She said nothing but tripped upstairs after breakfast and quickly shut the door of his room.

The next morning Hubert's mother had a little trouble shutting the door of his room and she noticed that Hubert had circles under his eyes as though he had not slept very well.

The next morning Hubert was very late coming downstairs and before he opened his door his mother heard a great clatter and scraping as though he were moving furniture. He had Little-Builder bolts stuck to his sweater and two paint pans in his hair. He was so sleepy he could barely keep his eyes open and he had a red mark on one cheek. His mother looked at it closely and saw that it was the shape and size of one of his stone blocks. He must have slept with his head on one of the bridges.

On the seventh day after Hubert's mother stopped putting away his toys, he did not come down to breakfast at all. About eleven o'clock his mother became worried and called up Mrs. Piggle-Wiggle.

She said, "Good Morning, Mrs. Piggle-Wiggle. This is the seventh day of the old-fashioned Won't-Pick-Up-Toys cure and I am worried. Hubert has not come downstairs at all this morning."

Mrs. Piggle-Wiggle said, "Let me see! The seventh day—it usually takes ten days—but Hubert has so many toys he would naturally be quicker."

"Quicker at what?" asked Hubert's mother anxiously.

"Quicker at getting trapped in his room" said Mrs. Piggle-Wiggle. "You see, the reason Hubert hasn't come downstairs is that he cannot get out of his room. Have you noticed anything different about him lately?"

"Well," said Hubert's mother, "he looks as though he hasn't been sleeping well and on the fourth morning he had a red blotch on his cheek just the shape of one of his stone blocks."

"Hmmmmm," said Mrs. Piggle-Wiggle. "He probably can't get at his bed and is sleeping with his head on his blocks for a pillow."

"But what will I do?" asked Hubert's mother. "How will I feed him?"

"Wait until he calls for food, then tell him to open the window and you put a piece of rather dry bread and peanut butter on the garden rake. He will have to drink out of the hose. Tie it to the rake and poke it up to him."

When Hubert's mother hung up the phone she heard a muffled shouting from the direction of Hubert's room. Hubert was shouting, "Mother, I'm hungry!"

His mother said, "Go over and open the window, dear. I will send something up to you on the rake."

Mrs. Prentiss took the crusty piece of a very old loaf of bread, spread some peanut butter on it and took it around to the side of the house. Pretty soon Hubert's window was raised about a foot and a hand and arm appeared. His mother stuck the bread on one of the tines of the rake and poked it up at the window. The hand groped around for a while and then found the bread and jerked it off. The window banged shut.

That night when Hubert's father came home his mother told him all about Mrs. Piggle-Wiggle's treatment. Hubert's father said, "Mrs. Piggle-Wiggle sounds all right, but none of this would have happened if Hubert's grandfather hadn't given him so many toys. When I was a boy all I needed to have a good time was a little piece of string and a stick. Why, I—"

Mrs. Prentiss said, "Not that old string-and-stick routine again, John. Anyway now that Hubert has the toys the picture has changed."

Mr. Prentiss hid his face behind the evening paper and said, "Something smells delicious. Is it Irish stew, I hope?"

"Yes, dear," said Hubert's mother worrying about how she was going to serve Irish stew to Hubert on a rake. She finally put a potato on one prong, a carrot on another, an onion on another and pieces of meat on the last three. The window was opened only about three inches but the hand grabbed the food. After dinner Hubert's father tied the hose to the rake and held it up while Hubert put his mouth to the window opening and tried to get a drink of water. It was not very successful but he managed to get a few drops.

Mrs. Prentiss was worried. The next morning she knocked on Hubert's door and said, "Hubert, what are you doing in there?"

Hubert said, "I've got a bear pen made out of bureau drawers and my bed's the mother bear's house and my train runs under my bed thirteen times now."

"Hubert, dear, don't you think you should try and come out soon?" asked his mother.

Hubert said, "I don't wanna come out. I like it in here. All my toys are out and I can play with them any old time I wanna. This is fun."

His mother went downstairs and called Mrs. Piggle-Wiggle. Mrs. Piggle-Wiggle said, "Oh, but he will want to come out. Wait and see."

That afternoon about two o'clock there was music on the street and children's voices laughing and calling and pretty soon, right past Hubert's house, marched Mrs. Piggle-Wiggle and all the children and right behind them came the circus parade. Hubert managed, by putting one foot in a bureau drawer and the other in a freight car of his train, to get up to the window and look out. He waved to Mrs. Piggle-Wiggle and she called, "Hurry, hurry, Hubert! We are going to march all over town and then we are all going to the circus."

Hubert turned around quickly with the idea of getting to the door and joining the fun, but the freight car went scooting under the bed and the bureau drawer tipped over and hit him smartly on the shins. Hubert began to cry and to try and kick his way to the door. But everything he kicked seemed to hit back. He kicked a building and a big block fell on his toe. He kicked at a Little-Builder office building and it fell over and clouted him on the back of the head. He kicked a book and it hit a lamp which fell and knocked a heavy wooden elephant off the bedpost onto Hubert's shoulder. He could hear the music of the circus parade growing fainter and fainter and so he bawled louder and louder.

Then he heard a tapping at his window. He crawled over and reached out. It was the rake with a note on it. He took the note and opened it. It said:

The only way you can get out of that trap is to put everything away where it belongs. If you hurry we will wait for you.

Your Friend,
Mrs. Piggle-Wiggle

Hubert began by finding the Little-Builder box. He took down an office building and put each piece in its right place. Then he put away the stone blocks, then the train tracks, the circus, the soldiers, the paints, the chemical set, the printing press, the books, the fire engines, the automobiles. He played little games, pretending that he was racing someone to see who could find the most parts of a game the quickest.

He had to take off the bedclothes and shake them in order to find the soldiers and the circus and then he thought that as long as the bedclothes were off anyway, he might as well make his bed. It was so lumpy when he finished he thought he had left some airplanes in it and took the covers off again and shook them. He made the bed again and this time it was neat and smooth. Hubert was proud.

He was under the desk finding the last piece of the Little-Builder when he heard the music again. He put the piece in the box, put the box in the closet and tore down the stairs and out the front door.

There they came, Mrs. Piggle-Wiggle, all the children and the CIRCUS! Hubert ran out to meet them and

43

nobody said anything about the pan of orange paint stuck in his hair or the word XYPGUN printed on his cheek in purple ink.

Away they went down the street, Hubert carrying the flag and yelling the loudest.

1. Hubert had several problems that led to disorganization. Although it is a fiction story, many of these problems parallel our situation as adults. Are any of the things that got Hubert into trouble problems you have?

   ___ Gifts from others
   ___ Too many belongings in general
   ___ Failure to put things back when used
   ___ Letting others mess up the organization of your room
   ___ Hoping help will come to rescue you.

2. Initially Hubert liked living in clutter. Do you like some parts of your house to be cluttered, to be surrounded by your belongings?

3. Hubert started being negatively impacted by his clutter (ink on his clothes, paint in his hair, sleeping on blocks, etc.). How does clutter negatively affect your life?

4. Mrs. Piggle-Wiggle's suggestion was to let the disorganization become so bad that Hubert would come to hate it. Is there some part of your house that is in that state or nearing it?

5. In the end, the desire to have fun, to have a good social life, changed Hubert's thinking and habits.

What would be the strongest appeal for you to change your cluttered way of life?

6. Hubert unrealistically organized his room in a very short time. How long do you think it would take to organize each room in your house that needs help?

List each room. Estimate how long each room will take to finish. You may not guess correctly, but just addressing the problem will be beneficial.

part 2

The Real World
of the Messie

3

"Say, Honey . . ."

How Men Fit In

Whether because of biology, culture, or just plain contrariness, men are different from women in many ways. That means that Messie men (and there are plenty of them, believe me!) have their own peculiar, male ways of proclaiming their disorganization to the world.

There doesn't seem to be as much pressure from society for men to be as organized as women. Think of all the "organizers" we provide for men—mothers for boys and young men, wives for married men, and secretaries for men at work. Two types of men have been traditionally excused from being organized at all—bachelors and absentminded-professor types. But what does that do to those of us who are disorganized, right-brain-dominant women? Not only are we expected to organize for ourselves but to keep the men around us organized too.

It might seem as though men have no trouble even if they are Messies because of the women who will take care of them. But beware! Sometimes the system breaks down in the following two cases:

1. The Messie man who lives alone. All over this country there are pockets of mass clutter perpetuated by men living alone. Unlike women, men are not schooled by their magazines and conversations with one another to strive for order and beauty. Many organized, high-style men maintain beautiful homes, but this is more of their own personal desire than societal pressure.

Those Messie single men are suffering pretty much alone. They are unable to enjoy coming home although they vehemently declare they can "relax" there. They are frustrated because they can't find things but know "It's here somewhere." Many will not allow anybody in the doors. Excluded friends and neighbors only suspect things may not be quite as they should be.

These men may rationalize their lifestyles to themselves and others by taking the macho approach ("Real men don't make beds"), the laid-back approach ("Hey, I'm comfortable"), or the psychological approach ("I've got to be me"). To a large extent, these single men are cut off from help except for an occasional mother or girlfriend who may take a stab at reform now and again.

Messies Anonymous is for men too. I really want to help them (in that macho, laid-back, moose-killing way that appeals to men, of course). *Playboy* magazine wanted some information about M.A. It would have been a great way to reach a lot of needy men, but I had to turn down their offer for my own ethical reasons. Too bad. You don't suppose *Field and Stream* or *Mechanics Illustrated* may someday be interested, do you?

2. *The married Messie who won't accept help from his wife or anybody else for that matter.* All over this country, there are also pockets of mass clutter perpetuated by married men who are driving their wives absolutely bonkers.

Compulsive about saving, they guard "their things" with zeal. The Messie man may have chosen an orderly wife to balance his own disorder, but now he won't let her function in "his" area. His area may be the garage, the junk room, his study, parts of the bedroom, or the whole house. His slogan is, "Leave that alone. I'll take care of it." Oh, if only this were true.

A woman is not likely to make much change in her man, especially if their relationship is not new. No person likes to be bullied, especially a man by a woman, so he resists her suggestions or tirades.

The only way any person will change is by seeing how very destructive his habits are to his own personal life and his relationships. He may suspect in a vague way that he is sabotaging his best life. It is the goal of this book to help crystallize this feeling and to show a way to make the change so sorely needed.

("Amen!" goes up the shout from a chorus of harried wives around the world.)

1. What would you say are the chief areas of clutter problem in your life?

2. What part have women played in keeping you organized? What part do they play now?

51

3. Do you negatively impact anyone in your life with your clutter? Do you take their distress seriously?

4. Are you willing to make necessary changes in your habits and life in order to clear up the clutter now there?

5. Make a plan to clear up your clutter. Include a time schedule.

4

"Hey, Mom . . ."

How Kids Fit In

Will children be in adult life what they are in childhood? Not necessarily. It is difficult to predict how a child will live as an adult. There are several different patterns children follow.

1. Pseudo Messie. Children try on different lifestyles to see which one they like. A flexible child who is not truly a Messie may, for a time, go into a disorderly disaster. That's part of what childhood is all about. Mother goes crazy and feels she must whip the kid into order when, in reality, if she just leaves him alone, like Hubert, he will see how tough it is to live as a Messie and will abandon it all by himself. The best way to move this kid along as quickly as possible is to ignore the chaos altogether or perhaps cooperate with it.

53

"Where do you want me to put this pile of clean clothes, son? Right here on the floor beside the ones I brought in last week? Fine."

After a little of this, the child who is not a true Messie will give it up and turn to the control he is fully capable of.

2. Messie Child/Cleanie Adult. Frequently moms will tell me about a child, usually a boy, who was not at all interested in order as a child, but now that he has his own place, he is "neat as a pin—won't let anybody put anything out of order." Apparently, this child felt adults were the orderly people, so when he was a child he let his adult mom do it. When he became an adult himself, he took over.

Sometimes a mom finds, to her amazement, that her impossibly Messie son is a different man with his new Cleanie wife. Studies have shown that when people are newly in love, they are a great deal more flexible and willing to change for the one they love. If the new wife can set up a satisfactory pattern early on in the marriage, she may be able to maintain order even after the newness of the relationship has worn off.

3. Cleanie Child/Messie Adult. There is also the child who is raised in a disorderly home with little order in her life, but she hopes that just as soon as she gets a place of her own, things will be different.

When Mary was a child, she was a bit absentminded and lost things a lot, but she managed to live a normally orderly life. As a young wife, she maintained a comfortable orderliness. As responsibility mounted and she added employment and children to her schedule, she floundered. Semi-Cleanie as a child, she was now a full-blown Messie, unable to maintain control under stress because she lacked a strong foundation from childhood. Like a house of cards, there comes a time when one more thing is too much, and the whole thing collapses.

The same kind of thing can happen to Johnny, who finds that the glut of paper he must handle as an adult, the rack of tools he needs, or the equipment and parts for his business overwhelm him. As a child, he could handle his baseball card collection and most of his school things, but now things are just too much.

4. *Messie Child/Messie Adult.* Some children are Messies as children, either because their moms are Messies who allow their children to be disorderly or because their moms, bless their hearts, try unsuccessfully to change their Messie child but cannot.

As adults, nothing is important enough to encourage them to change their lifestyles, and they continue on in the same pattern.

My approach with a disorganized child is to try to help the child maintain a level we can both be comfortable with. Many Messie kids really appreciate and need guidance, help, and training because they *can't* organize by themselves, and they know it.

All parents have different managerial styles. My style is to insist that the child not mess up the public areas of the house or anybody else's room. However, if after I have used all my help and influence, his room is still disorderly, I let it go, at least temporarily. When things get too bad or he seems more receptive later, I may return to the task. To me, it's not beneficial to nag, shout, and harass so much that the kid's life and our relationship is a shambles for the sake of an orderly room. For more help with training children to be organized, read *Neat Mom, Messie Kids* (Sandra Felton).

> Kids really appreciate guidance . . . because they can't organize by themselves.

Remember, too, that what you may be tempted to classify as a Messie symptom may be no more than normal childhood habits. "Things" are important to children, and they begin to collect at an early age: baseball cards, dolls, marbles, comic books, animals—both living and dead. Instead of banning collecting, help your child learn to keep it in check.

5. *Cleanie Child/Cleanie Adult.* There are some children so orderly that they cleaned themselves up as they came from the womb and have been at it ever since.

So important is order to them that they never experiment with another lifestyle and maintain a strictly organized approach in the face of all pressures not to do so.

> "It is easier to rule a kingdom than to regulate a family."
>
> —Japanese Proverb

This person must have order to function. With her it is not negotiable. She may live as a child in a household of Messies, but her room, or the part of the room that is hers, is perfect.

Although opposites do attract and we do choose mates to balance off our personalities (including the housekeeping area sometimes), when a nonnegotiating, hard-core Cleanie meets a nonnegotiating, hard-core Messie, something's got to give—sometimes it's the marriage.

Final thoughts: It is next to impossible to predict with certainty how a child will turn out in adulthood because we don't know what causes him to be the way he is now or what will influence him as an adult.

I greatly admire those household-manager moms who seem to be able to keep all twelve of their children, neat ones and messy ones alike, in orderly rooms without fussing or using the torture rack. I wish I were one. But since I'm not, I have to follow my priorities in the light of my own abilities. My approach is that I want a reasonably neat child with a reasonable amount of attention from me. *Reasonable* is a relative term, so it varies from person to person and from day to day.

56

I always thought that when the kids grow up and are out of the home, I will finally have time to muster up my organization, and have my home in perfect order, a dream I've had for 25 years! And guess what? It didn't happen. My habits are in my psyche, and although I've pursued methods through the years, or the easiest way to get the job of housework done efficiently, no method has ever stuck . . . so I want to change my ways after reading the Messie Manual, fix and paint everything, and FOR ONCE, be on top.

Do you know, I've been in charge of my own home for 25 years, and aside from occasional hints to make certain household chores easier, while coffee-klatching with other mothers, and our sharing and complaining, NOBODY has ever confessed in depth, that there's a difference between Cleanie and Messie housekeepers . . and I know I was different from the Cleanies, but as my self-esteem was always on the verge of bottoming out, it was so personal, I couldn't share it with anyone . . . but accept the endless treadmill of housework. And I longed so to make it easier, but didn't know how.

Thank you, Sandra Felton, for a shot of enthusiasm to this tired middle-aged Messie. You described me in a way nobody ever has, and I thank you for guiding the way out.

Carol / Minnesota

5

Not That Convenient

The Stress of Modern Technology

Let's face it, what we really want is for that man and those kids to help more. Here we are breaking our necks, and there's George, watching the New York Gnats attack the Seattle Skinks which, of course, he cannot forgo. He would like to skip some of these incredibly important TV happenings because he does believe in helping out around the house, but it is also part of his manly responsibility to keep up with the flow of current events.

Somehow the kids, bless them, take after their father with many similar cultural involvements—homework, band, ballet, and ball practice. Being responsible people, they have little time for helping around the house.

58

Of course, they do help *some*. But the fact remains that we, the wives and mothers, are incredibly busy—and harried and exhausted and frustrated and sometimes angry.

There are real reasons for these feelings. Running a house involves three "task packages": (1) making a living; (2) keeping house; and (3) taking care of the children.

Traditionally, the husband made the living, the wife kept house. George did help outside by mowing, cleaning gutters, and barbecuing. Mom brought up the children with evening and weekend input from Dad.

What Happened to Mom's Time?

Now with modern technology, however, the woman's job has become easier, and she can go to work outside the home without an adverse effect on housekeeping and child rearing. Right?

Wrong! A close look at the facts will show that modern technology is not the savior of woman's time it would seem to be. Initially, with the advent of technology, the time spent in women's work actually *increased* from 1920 to 1967. The amount of time spent in cooking did decrease, but that decrease was more than made up for by an increase in the time used for marketing, keeping records, doing laundry, and other jobs.

Why did this happen? Women who got nice washers and dryers actually spent a few hours a week more on laundry than women did before washing machines were common because they washed more often and because they didn't hire a "laundry lady" to help do the work.

The groceries used to be delivered by delivery boys, as did medicines from the pharmacy. The piano teacher came to the home. In smaller communities, the kids could walk to school. Doctors made house calls. Crime was less so kids could walk to the store for Mom and ride their bikes to a friend's house instead of Mom chauffeuring them around in the car. Mom didn't generally have a car, either.

With the advent of the two-car family, Mom was free to ferry the kids everywhere and then wait for them. She had to do her own laundry since it was now so easy (or seemed that way). What excuse did she have? She had to get her own groceries at convenient, new supermarkets. The vacuum bag needed changing along with the air-conditioner filter. The food processor dismantled a cabbage in no time flat, but then somebody had to dismantle the processor and clean it. When we opened the door to technology, additional work sneaked in behind. Work did become easier—but it took more time.

In 1965, women aged twenty-five to forty-four spent forty-six hours a week doing housework. Reports indicate that the time women spend doing housework has been dropping steadily in the last thirty-five years. Today women report spending about three hours a day on housework.

Why this drop has occurred is not clear. A large part of the reason may be because so many women work outside the home. When a married woman works outside the home, she spends fewer hours a week doing housework. Another reason may be because women have begun to adjust their time to the demands of technology.

How has all of this affected Dad and the kids?

How the Kids Fit In

Let's look at what has happened to the kids' place in the housework first. Around the turn of the century, the role of children in the home began to change. (You

60

didn't know we were going to delve into history, did you?) Up until this time, adults and kids of all classes except the gentry toiled more or less side by side to keep the household going. There was wood to gather, chop, and bring in. There was water to fetch. Kids were welcomed as workers into this people-powered world. Hardworking little rascals trudged through the blizzard to get the old Doc for the family down with the plague, saving them all. Now we use the phone to call the doctor. Brave little Peter was sent through the dark woods at night to get a hot coal from a neighbor because the fire had failed at his house and everyone was freezing to death. Now we flick a switch to get heat. Little Red Riding Hood took care of Grandma, and Heidi took care of goats. Now we send Grandma to a hospital and Heidi off to school. In short, in the past, children worked as an integral part of the family and took their chances with danger, trouble, and fatigue like everybody else.

> Around the turn of the century the role of children in the home began to change.

Conveniences such as gas, running water, and electricity increasingly allowed people to take an emotionally sentimental approach to children. People gave birth to children in order to enjoy them. A child's contribution to the home was largely aesthetic or pleasurable. They were no longer expected to work as they had previously. Good moms "took care" of children in a way not done before.

Today, a family with one child aged six to eleven averages half an hour of work a day from that child. A child from twelve to seventeen does a tad more than one hour of work a day in a one-child family. If there is more than one child in the home, the work gets spread out so each child has to do slightly less than the only child.

Today, 15 percent of household work is carried out by the kids, but they require more maintenance than the work they perform.

What is Dad's Place?

A good husband performs about 15 percent of the work around the house, but he also requires more than that for maintenance. Even if the man of the house loses his job and his wife continues to work, that 15 percent share rises very little. This is the time when he least wants to begin to do "women's work." His own self-image is already weak enough.

All of this leaves—you guessed it—70 percent or more for the wife to do in most homes.

Why don't the men do more? Women, especially working women, are being worn down by the stress of overwork. In the last ten years, even though many married women have poured into the work force, men have only slightly increased their help around the house.

Let's look again at how this came about. As technology moved in and the actual amount of time a woman spent on housework increased, children began to do less and less housework by general agreement. In their defense, children did have more education to deal with than their pioneer counterparts, who shouldered more of the household chores. Dad, who held down a full-time job and did some work at home, still contributed more actual total work time to the family than Mom did. In the mid-sixties, Dad did about sixty-four hours total work, and Mom did about sixty-three hours of total work. (Total work includes all three of the task packages including work outside the home.)

Let's face it, in many upper-middle-class homes in "the old days," the woman had it easy. She had a leisurely way of life, whiling away her hours tatting in the sunroom, arranging flowers, giving teas, joining clubs, and preparing for her husband's return, at which time she could minister to his needs by bringing him his slippers, pipe, and paper. Anybody who works all day at the office or factory needs pampering, she thought.

Who Brings Mom Slippers, Pipe, and Paper?

Now, along with the man, the woman may work all day (52 percent do), rush home, and try to bring some order and beauty and food to her household. Nobody, man or woman, no matter how hard he or she works, gets pampered today. In the recent shift, the woman who used to do an average of sixty-three hours total work now may do forty hours work outside the home or more plus the thirty-five or so hours of housework, making a total of seventy-five to eighty hours of total work. Then, of course, follow all of the other things like PTA, teacher conferences, clothes shopping, haircuts, trips to the vet, and so on. The wonder is that women have survived at all.

Men did not generally complain about their work load even when the scale was tipped heavily in favor of women as it was in the past. The men were working at a comfortable level as far as time use was concerned (we're talking average here), and they were supported at home by their wives. Working women today are stretched way beyond the comfortable level of time use (eighty hours or so a week for many when outside work and housework are combined), and there is nobody to support Mom with slippers, pipe, and paper when she gets home. What

Working women today are stretched way beyond the comfortable level of time use.

> "The term 'working mother' is redundant."
>
> —Erma Bombeck

she needs is a "wife." But instead, it's "Mom, are my jeans washed? What's for supper?"

Making Changes in Your Favor

What can a woman do about this dismal state of affairs? If she is a Messie who has trouble getting her household rolling under any circumstances and who has gone to work outside the home to (a) earn more money for the family; (b) get away from the frustration of the house; (c) succeed; or (d) all of the above, there are several things she can do.

1. Remove the rose-colored glasses. Many women never slow down enough to realize what a stressful situation modern women are in. They think they can bring home the bacon, fry it up in a pan, and still be a beautiful, sexy lover that evening. The sentiment, "I am woman; I am invincible," does not work well on the day-to-day housekeeping level. It's more like, "I am woman; I am exhausted."

2. Make changes in your favor. Whether you are married or not, employed or not, have kids or not, the truth is that many women, especially Messies, have more to do than they can comfortably cope with. Many are drowning. Be alert to every opportunity for changes that will make your life easier. Then make them, even if it means transferring extra jobs to reluctant family members.

3. Simplify wherever possible. This can be done by setting up a convenient base to work from, which means living as close to job, grocery store, doctors, schools, and piano teachers as possible. I know that the best piano teacher lives far away or the best doctor is worth a very long trip. That is your choice, of course, but except in very unusual circumstances, there are probably good ones closer to you. You might be surprised. It also helps

64

to live where older children can walk to the library, sports facilities, and stores. (Making the change is painful, but continuing this strung-out way of life is painful also.)

4. *Use all the help available.* Messies are uncommonly generous about not bothering other people. If the bottled-water man comes to a Messie's house, she will say, "Just put the bottle there in the living room," to save him the trouble of carrying it, even if her kitchen is presentable. A Cleanie would have him bring it all the way in—no extra work for her and certainly no water bottle cluttering the living room even for a minute.

Messies are always willing to run errands for others but very unwilling to ask others to run errands for them. When this point was raised at a recent M.A. self-help group, a voice piped up, "Do you suppose that's because Messies really have a low opinion of themselves?" "Yes!" came the spontaneous response from everyone in the room.

Consider this. Studies show that the more money a woman makes on her job, the more her husband helps around the house. Notice that it is not how much *time* she spends at work but how much *money* she makes. It seems that as her time becomes more valuable at work, it also is seen to be more valuable at home. What does this say about the woman who doesn't work outside the home and makes no money at all? Does her time have no value at all? Is that why she is asked to do the errands, pick up after people, and so on? Perhaps she is willing to accept all of the overflow others don't want to do because she doesn't place much value on her time either.

> Organizational techniques are the shock absorbers of life.

Consider this also. Sociologists Philip Blumstein and Pepper Schwartz in their book *American Couples* report that men are doing slightly more housework than they did ten years ago, but the more housework the husband does, the more the couple fight about it. This adds stress to the relationship between the husband and wife. Obviously, willing help is not always easy to get, although in 15 percent of marriages, there is equality in division of housework, and many husbands do a great deal to adjust and help out the swamped wife.

5. *Organize.* The problems of overwork apply to most women today, but they apply more directly to Messies who have enough trouble juggling a normally stressful life, much less the incredible schedules modern choices have put us into.

Organizational techniques are the shock absorbers of life. The ones used in this book can help a whale of a lot to smooth life out to the point where it is a comfortable ride. Use them.

A word of caution is in order. Do not use organizational techniques to stack your life full of more activities. The first order of life is *simplify.* Then organize your life into a meaningful flow.

Life should be like a Japanese flower arrangement—a few significant pieces skillfully handled. Instead, we too often choose the English country-garden approach—full, wild, and random.

Finally, the bottom line is this: People today should be very careful of the commitments they make for themselves and their families because modern life requires a deceptively large amount of time and effort to carry out family goals. Once those goals are set, however, every member of the family should try—out of love and fairness—to work together toward an enjoyable and

> "Cleanliness is not next to godliness. It isn't even in the same neighborhood. No one has ever gotten a religious experience out of removing burned-on cheese from the grill of the toaster oven."
>
> —Erma Bombeck

full life for everyone in the family, especially Mom, who is caught in many cases at this time in history, in an especially pressured situation.

1. Describe your thoughts and feelings about the amount of work you do, especially in relation to the amount of work done by others in the family. Is it well balanced?

2. List the names of people in your household. Beside each name list one job you could transfer to them (after proper training, of course.)

3. Are there any changes you can make in your life, such as establishing a car pool or dropping an activity?

   If you were to make a change, what might that change be?

   If you were to drop one activity, what might that activity be?

4. If you hesitate to share activities with others or to simplify, what is the reason you think might contribute to that hesitation? Are you willing to question whether it is a wise reason to keep? Are you willing to abandon it?

5. If someone asks you to help her and you feel it is an imposition you should not participate in, will you be willing to say *no* when you would previously have said *yes*? Can you think of an example that might arise?

part 3

From the Inside Out

6

Hidden Beauty

Very Hidden

"Beauty" is not a concept that rises easily to the surface of the reforming Messie's mind. "Survival" is a more appropriate idea. It was not always that way. When we first got married, we dreamed of the wonderful house we would have. When that first apartment or house became a reality, our dreams swelled into pure fantasy.

We searched for our style, different from our mothers', of course. French provincial, early American, modern, art deco—what would it be? Until we had time or money or figured out what we wanted for ourselves, we would settle for that catch-all style called eclectic.

Somewhere, somehow, out there in the future, we knew in our hearts there was a beautiful house that we would create. The extension of a woman's personality is her home, and what a wonderful home ours would be. Messies are, after all, generally idealistic, quality people. Many have artistic tendencies and love art and crafts.

Then came the reality of living. All those dreams began to fray around the edges until there were only a few strands left.

We may have some of the pieces of furniture we dreamed of and a few of the accessories, but mostly the dream is crushed under the shoes in the living room or buried under the books piled around the bed.

We begin to question our dream. Perhaps we dreamed it wrong. We feel we need an interior decorator. Occasionally, we buy a lovely new spread and curtains for our bedroom, but it just doesn't work. In the store and in our minds it sparkled brightly, but in our house the beauty dims among the overabundance of furniture holding the overabundance of pictures, electrical gadgets, and possessions, all of which are useful and clutter the beauty right out of existence.

Actually, the beauty is there. It has just been obscured.

Actually, the beauty is there. It has just been obscured. Under the overlay, you have a lovely house. All you need to do is remove what is obscuring it, and you will be surprised what emerges. Remember, the beautiful house is there already. You just need to reveal it.

Now, let's see how to find the beauty.

We must know what we are looking for in order to find it. I well remember the stress I was under when I first began my search. It had been so long since I had dared to dream that I could hardly remember what my dream had been. I had begun to clear away the clutter, but I didn't know what beauty to expect to find underneath. I didn't know what my style was, what beauty I wanted.

Beatitudes for Messies

Blessed is the Messie who is able to hope after years of failure that a new way of life exists for her.

Blessed is the Messie who forgives herself for years wasted in messy living and the joys she and her family have lost because of it.

Blessed is the Messie who is able to persevere in the changing process when the pressure of modern life and her own natural tendencies make going back to the old ways appealing.

Blessed is the Messie who, in her disorder, retains a vision of the order, beauty, and peace available to her in her house.

Blessed is the Messie who finds the courage to begin again when the house has slipped out of control and vision grows dim.

Blessed is the Messie who understands when the family doesn't cooperate that they did not necessarily come to the point of change exactly when she did.

Blessed is the family who cooperates "for Mom's sake," even though her new goals for the house may not be significant to them at the time it is to her.

Blessed is the Messie who realizes that laughter and love are a big part of a meaningful home. Laughter and love are what have gotten her and her family through the old messy times and they will add grace to the new and better organized life.

In search of my dream, I began to thumb through decorator magazines. It was a Sunday afternoon. I began to wonder if I had no style, when to my surprise a beautiful page came into view. A lush green carpet, a French provincial chair, custom molding on the light green wall. Like a spark revitalizing my vision, I realized that I did know beauty. Quickly, picture in hand, I went to the living room. Holding up the picture I envisioned the room—where the chair would be, how we could place the molding, the lush green carpeting. I still have the picture five years later, and my living room has undergone quite a change. It's not green or French provincial, but it is a lot better and growing more beautiful every day.

How can you use this story in accomplishing your dreams?

First, you have to make your dream concrete. That's what the picture did for me. It crystallized my dream. You can do that too by flipping through magazines until you find the picture of your dream room. Don't get carried away and fill a whole scrapbook with pictures. Find one—or four at the most—so your dream will be well focused. Put the picture in a frame and hang it on your wall. Beside it put an empty frame of the same size with a piece of blank, white paper in it. In that empty picture frame, low at the bottom in a box, write a date. Don't make it too soon because you've undoubtedly got far to go. Put a much later date if you need to, but don't omit the date just because you are afraid you'll miss it.

The empty picture frame is where you will put the picture you take of your house when your dream comes true. The date is on the bottom so that it won't obscure the vision of the beauty you will create.

In *Guideposts* magazine, Jeanette Doyle Parr tells a story that encouraged her during her husband's lingering illness. A poor young man in Mississippi wanted to leave the plantation for the city and better opportunity, but it

Once upon a midnight dreary,
There I stood, my eyes all bleary.
'Mid coffee cup and Twinkie wrapper—
How I yearned to be a midnight napper!

But once upon a morning bright,
I'd vowed to clean before the night.
Though ambition fled before the noon,
I still refused to change my tune.

Once upon a dawn less dreary,
My whole house shone, spotless and cheery.
And though no one would know but I,
I claimed a victory with my sigh . . .

. . . and woke the kids for breakfast.

seemed hopeless. After hearing a backwoods evangelist paint an inspiring picture of faith as "evidence of things not seen," John decided that what he needed was some "evidence" for his faith. He found an empty fruit jar and put it under his bed. That would be his evidence. Each time he got an extra odd job, he put the money in his evidence jar. He filled the jar many times before he could leave for the city. There he married and got work with the railroad.

One day, John bought a picture frame with a cardboard backing and hung it over a crack in the plaster of their apartment. That was where the deed to their home would hang one day. When each child was born, he hung two empty frames, one for his high school diploma and one for his college diploma. At the writing of the story, thirteen frames had been hung and nine filled. Two children were in college, and one was a senior in high school.

John said that when our sights begin to slip, we need some evidence to keep our faith on track.

That's what our empty frame is, an "evidence" frame to keep our goal in mind down the long path to fulfillment. It helps us to remember that the beauty really is already there for us to discover.

One more thing is important about that empty frame with the white paper in it. Make a border around the outside of the white paper, inside the frame, in your favorite color. Use colored pens and crayons or colored paper. How you make it is unimportant. Evidence in education suggests that a border of our favorite color intensifies our attention and concentration. The colored border will help you along your way to success.

> Slowly, day after day and year after year, a pile of rocks took form, and from these, a castle began to rise.

My husband is from the Florida Keys. Not long ago, he took me to a beautiful spot overlooking the Atlantic Ocean to see what he called the "rock castle" and told me the story of how it was built. To understand this story, you need to know that the Keys are covered with multitudes of different-sized rocks made from pieces of coral. These rocks are a nuisance to live with, interfering with yard work now and with farming in the days when lime groves flourished on the Keys. However, one man saw potential in this situation and instructed his family to always bring back a rock in each hand when they came in from the lime grove. Slowly, day after day and year after year, a pile of rocks took form, and from these, a castle began to rise. Now overlooking the Atlantic, surrounded by swaying palms and a carpet of dark green grass, is a castle of coral rock.

The rocks were there for everyone to pick up freely, but only one person had the vision. From that vision, held persistently over the years, the dream became reality.

Your house is like that spot on the Keys. There is a beautiful castle there if you have the vision for it, and the means to that beauty is not far out of your reach. It takes vision, imagination, and persistence to find it. Remember, the beauty is already there. All you need to do is uncover it.

> "If you want a golden rule that will fit everybody, this is it: Have nothing in your houses that you do not know to be useful or believe to be beautiful."
>
> —Walter Kitteredge

1. Describe when you first began to dream what your house would be. Was it when you were very small? When you were a teenager? Getting your first apartment? When you were first engaged or married? Later?

2. Describe your dream at that time.

3. What style appeals to you? If you don't know exactly, describe the house of a friend or a model home you admire.

4. What colors are used in this house, and how?

5. What is your favorite color?

6. Where will you locate a decorator magazine to look at?

7. Where will you get the frames to hang on the wall? If at a store, which one?

8. When will you get the frames?

9. Where in your house will you hang the two frames?

Right away you know that I am a "true Messie" by the faint type. Can't give up this old ribbon just yet. If I strike the keys hard enough I can get just a few more letters off it!

On the evening of May 17th this year my friend Elaine shared her set of your tapes with me. I listened intently and took notes like crazy! I laughed and cried as I recognized myself as you described a Messie.

Fortunately I had a new notebook handy and I put my notes in it. Since than I have worked from those notes. I followed your instructions exactly. Within a couple of days things began to look different and I was acting differently and my husband said to me, "What in the world has happened to you?" and I replied, "I have discovered what a lovely, intelligent, creative, artistic, energetic, etc., etc., person I am." And he said, "How did you discover that?" Then I told him about your tapes.

Actually by the time I finished listening to your tapes my attitude about myself had changed and that is a miracle! I really felt good about myself for the first time in my life that I can remember, that is really deep down good about myself (I am 56 years old). It made all the difference in the world in my attitude about myself and my housework. Now that I know that I'm really not lazy I can get things done!

Thank you, thank you, thank you for being brave enough to start Messies Anonymous. It's a wonderful thing! Many women will profit greatly from your willingness to share your discoveries. I am most grateful.

Norine / Ohio

7

A New Vision

See Yourself a Successful Housekeeper

The reason we have placed such emphasis on envisioning a beautiful house is that our goal must be definite, consistent, and intense in order to work.

You have already begun to set your beautiful-house goal and to take steps to cement it firmly in your mind.

Equally important is for you to see yourself as a successful housekeeper. How do we do this?

There is some danger in calling our organization Messies Anonymous because it suggests a negative thought about ourselves. The name has its advantages, however, and so it stands.

At a recent M.A. self-help support group, the leader encouraged the participants to give themselves positive descriptive names such as

Neat Nancy (that one was easy)
or Marvelous-Housekeeper Mary
or Successful Sam
or Throwaway Tina

This is the approach we need to take once we have accepted ourselves as having a real problem that we are determined to change.

1. Look for the neat, orderly person in you. Obviously, there is more to you than the messy side or you would not be reading this book, seeking a change. The side of you that loves order and beauty is what encourages you to change. I believe it is a mistake to think of ourselves as two different people, one messy and one neat, because this fragments our approach. The more integrated our approach, the more we are living in harmony with our whole selves, the more successful we will be. Look for the successful housekeeper part of yourself that has been ignored or lost for a long time. She (or he) really is there. It is this side of you that needs to be integrated into your functioning.

> Look for the successful housekeeper part of yourself.

In order to encourage this side of yourself, answer these questions *as a successful, house-under-control person would* by circling the best, appropriate letter. Your neat part will know just which one to circle.

  1. When I come home from shopping I
      a. put my things in the bedroom to be put away later.
      b. drop my things by the door and rest.
      c. put away my purchases before going on to another activity.

2. When I take off my shoes I
    a. usually leave them where I took them off and forget them.
    b. leave them where I took them off and put them away when I go to the bedroom.
    c. immediately put them in the bedroom closet.

3. After dinner I
    a. clear the table, wash the dishes, and clear the kitchen.
    b. leave the dishes on the table until I feel like getting to them.
    c. take the dishes to the kitchen to wash later.

4. When I get up in the morning, I
    a. make the bed as soon as it is unoccupied.
    b. leave the bed unmade for a long time (to air out, etc.).
    c. never make the bed (I have good reasons).

5. Concerning books, newspapers, and magazines, I
    a. never allow books, magazines, or newspapers to accumulate to such a point that they interfere with a lovely house.
    b. hate to do it, but I keep books, magazines, and papers moving out so that things aren't too stacked.
    c. can't get rid of any books or magazines, and I keep the papers around at least a few days.

6. In my closets, I have
   a. clothes worn regularly and clothes from the past that are never worn.
   b. only those clothes that are worn regularly.
   c. clothes both past and present and other clothes I am just storing.

7. In the area of storage, I have
   a. things stored away easily because I don't keep too much. They are easy to find and easy to get to.
   b. many things put away and many things stored out in living areas as well. I don't have enough storage space.
   c. everything packed into some containers or drawers or under the bed. They are hard to get to or to find but they are out of sight pretty much.

8. When I come home at night, I find my house to be
   a. lovely and hospitable—a place of rest because it is orderly and beautiful.
   b. depressing because it is cluttered. It wears me out to try to live there.
   c. functional—it's no great burden, but it's no great pleasure either.

2. Accept yourself. Several of the chapters in this book do not emphasize how to organize the house but instead deal with understanding and accepting ourselves as we are, messy house and all. Once that base is established, we can move on.

"The desire to change carries within it the seeds of its own fulfillment."

—Napoleon Hill

3. *Forget the past.* Dorothea Brande tells how she stumbled on an idea that changed her life. She decided she would act as if she could not fail by forgetting or ignoring past failures. Instead of just hoping for success, she would assume that powers and abilities that would enable her to succeed were there and act as if they were. Shortly, she was succeeding at her goal—producing and selling her writing.

> "Habit is habit, and not to be flung out the window by any man but coaxed downstairs a step at a time."
>
> —Mark Twain

You assume that the power and ability to gain complete control over your house are there and then act on that assumption—"act as if." They are there, you know.

The mind cannot live with inconsistency. If you keep the assumption that you have the power and ability to succeed running strong in your mind by concentrating on your goal, all that talk about how you never will get control of the house will tuck tail and slink right out of your thoughts.

4. *Use emotion to stimulate success.* Messies are generally an easy-going lot. That is one reason we put up with so much for so long where others, especially Cleanies, would have taken a stand long ago.

It was anger that propelled me into change when my kitchen sink sprang a leak and destroyed my cabinets before I knew it because of the clutter under the sink.

Perhaps you are angry. Anger is a bright, sharp emotion that works well for change. Perhaps you are disgusted and agitated. If so, use the energy of those emotions to make the change.

Perhaps you can use the emotion of intense desire or love of beauty to help you begin moving in the direction of success for your house.

84

Whatever emotion you find within you, encourage that emotion in yourself. For too long we thought there was little hope for our houses, and so we muffled those feelings because they only added to our frustration.

5. *Don't get keyed up.* Once we establish our goals and are assured that we are perfectly capable of accomplishing them and find emotion to propel us along, we no longer have to struggle. A quiet, consistent, controlled determination will cut away at the job until it is done. The blowtorch does not spray out its flame freely in all directions. All of that heat is focused and controlled down to a blue-hot flame point that knifes by its concentration into the job at hand.

Have you ever noticed the detached approach Cleanies take when they get busy in the house? You can see it on their faces. In some sense they seem to switch off their minds and let their bodies do the work. Cleanies are more determined than Messies, but they are less involved. This more impersonal approach is what frees them up to work efficiently. Perhaps it enables them to work for longer periods, too, because their minds are elsewhere and not on the clock.

Several Messies have written and told me they are professional cleaners and temporary office help who are highly successful in their work and much in demand because of their efficiency. At home, however, they are unable to get control. Why? They are too involved in a personal way with their homes.

It relieves us of a lot of pressure when we realize we do not have to get in a dither about the house. Step back, way back, in a detached manner from the job in front of you and then quietly and deliberately set to work. Don't try harder. Try differently.

In *Psycho-Cybernetics* (Wilshire Book Co.), Maxwell Maltz reports that Pavlov, on his deathbed, was asked to leave a final word to his students about how they could succeed. He said three words: "Passion and gradualness."

No headlong rush to success—slow but sure does the trick.

6. *Ignore hindrances.* I'm not saying to pretend there are no hindrances. I am saying not to let them stand in the way of accomplishing your goal. Sometimes the hindrance is lack of money, sometimes lack of energy, sometimes lack of time, sometimes lack of knowledge. But somehow, if all the facets of success are set in motion, we attract the answers to our problems.

Get started as though there were no hindrances, and you will be surprised at how the problems solve themselves.

7. *Use springboards to success.* Your house is not all bad. There are parts of it that are very good. Emphasize the lovely parts and work from there. Mary Crowley, founder of Home Interiors, told stories of how one spot of beauty in the house could spark discouraged homemakers into creating a house glowing with beauty. If you have a lovely coffee table, shine it brightly, decorate it nicely. Many have found inspiration in a clean sink. Choose a spot that will act as a springboard to order and beauty in the whole house.

1. If you were to give yourself a positive nickname, what would it be?

2. Complete this sentence three different ways to show what a successful housekeeper does. Example: A successful housekeeper uses her family to help keep things under control.

   A successful housekeeper:
   a.
   b.
   c.

3. The emotion I am going to use to spur success
   is . . .
   Explain.

4. What springboards to success are you going to
   use in your house?

I keep a tablet in the kitchen and as I use a product
(like a can of tomato sauce), I add it to the buying
list. I always keep one jar of mayonnaise in the
cupboard and one in the refrigerator. Then when I
take the one out of the cupboard to put into the
refrigerator, I add it to the list.

My husband also writes on the list whenever he uses
an item. He will add things like light bulbs and
cleaning supplies. He particularly enjoys the list
because he gets his favorite foods (by simply adding
them to the list) without continually reminding me.

When our boy grows up, I'll teach him to do the same
and his reward will be a special item that he wants
from the grocery store. I can hardly wait!

Tina

Games We Play

And How to Win

Having a messy house is painful. It is hard to know why this is so. Why can't a person relax, be messy, and actually enjoy it? I see two reasons:

- the nerve-wracking feeling of losing control and
- the loss of self-esteem a person experiences when her house is not pretty.

Order and beauty are the twins of self-esteem.

Prescott Lecky, a psychologist who did much work in this area, put it this way. He said that almost everyone has two strong beliefs that control them:

1. The feeling that they can do their part to contribute in their own unique way.
2. The feeling that their dignity should be held intact.

Having a messy house we are unable to control consistently brings us frustration and humiliation, and that flies in the face of both of these key beliefs.

Because being a Messie makes us feel bad, we try to dull the pain by playing several diversionary games. The creative Messie uses all of these tactics on a regular basis as needed.

1. Avoid the house. One of the simplest ways to avoid the pain of an unpleasant house is to leave it and busy oneself elsewhere. Shopping meets the need well. The beauty-loving Messie is able to surround herself with beautiful new things in the department store or interesting things at the antique store or garage sale. There always is the hope that somewhere out there may be just the thing to really perk up the house. So we drag home our treasures and clutter more surfaces or fill more closets and drawers. In addition, this pastime can become very expensive.

We can go out to the park or visit friends to get away. Or we can go to work, either on volunteer projects or for profit. Both of these solutions, while personally or economically satisfying, keep the Messie out of the house and away from solving the problems there.

2. Find distraction in the house. Some women do not leave the house physically. They do so mentally, however, by reading books, watching TV (especially soaps, which often have lovely, orderly homes), and getting caught up in hobbies or other projects. Some people sleep too much. Dreams are preferable to the reality surrounding us.

3. Change the definition and description of the condition of the house. So that we don't feel so bad, we sometimes change the description of the house from, "The house is a wreck," to, "This is the house of a busy person," or, "This is the house of a person who is canning." That way the spotlight is turned away from the messy house to something more positive.

4. Change the source of our bad feeling away from the house. This is perhaps most commonly done by saying to ourselves in all sincerity, "I feel bad. What could it be that makes me feel that way? It must be the children. They are so noisy and active. It is my husband. He doesn't appreciate me."

We can turn on our family and attack them for their faults rather than take the responsibility for our bad feelings about the condition of the house.

5. Change the appraisal. "It really isn't so bad. I like a house that looks lived in. I can find things better this way. I know where everything is. It's a sign of genius."

By changing how we judge the disorganization, we feel a little better for a little while about how the house looks.

6. Overdo planning and doing. When things reach a head and we feel we must face the facts about the situation, it sometimes helps us to begin to plan how we are going to remedy things. Sometimes this takes the form of much talk or of daydreams about what we should do.

On other occasions, the hurting Messie will fall into the work with the zeal of a Tasmanian devil, snapping and growling the house into form. Then she says to herself, "I did my part," as the house slowly slides into chaos again.

7. Overthrow the feeling. When it becomes unpleasant to live with our bad feelings, we sometimes kick over the traces and ignore the feelings altogether by saying, "I don't care. This is me! I'm not going to care anymore."

Of course, all of these approaches work for a while but not very well or for very long. That's why we switch from one approach to another.

Actually our efforts should not be spent in playing games to ease the pain we feel about the house but in relieving the thing that causes us the pain—the messy house itself. That's the only game we win.

In order to do that, however, we need to stop telling ourselves that we don't care about the house, that it looks lived in, that it is the children and husband who are at fault. We need to stop avoiding the pain by sleeping or reading or leaving. Let's tell ourselves the real truth about the house and ourselves.

> "The best way to escape from a problem is to solve it."
>
> —Brendan Francis

Let's look at the house first. Johnny Carson used to say, "The house is *so* bad . . ." and the audience would shout, "How bad is it?" Answer that question for yourself without overexaggerating or overgeneralizing. It is *not* 100 percent bad—not awful.

Check one of the following.

The state of the house is:

__moderately good, but in some need of improving.
__moderately poor, but it has obvious good points.
__poor.
__extremely poor.

Let's turn to the specific rooms of the house and list them in order of their need for order and beauty. List the room that is the neediest first and go down to the least needy.

1.
2.
3.
4.
5.
6.
7.
8.

Now, you see, the fact they are not all on the top line shows that the picture is not all dark.

Messies like to use broad brushes and paint everything the same. It is for this reason that we must stop and evaluate things specifically.

Just as it is true that the house is not 100 percent bad, your control of it is not totally gone. Let's search for reality in that area too.

List three of your best points as you relate to the house—three things you do that contribute well to the house.

1.
2.
3.

Now list three things that you do that add to the disorder of the house.

1.
2.
3.

Now, let's go one step further in objectively evaluating the state of the house.

Check the statement you feel is true.

__I absolutely must have a beautiful, orderly house.

__It is preferable for me to have a lovely, self-assuring house.

__I don't need a nice house. I do perfectly well without it.

The middle statement is true. It is preferable to get your house under control, but it is not absolutely necessary. If you convince yourself that it is a "must," you will freeze up your objective perspective. Only the truth will free you to make progress.

> Messies are folks of mixed extremes and so find themselves caught in contradictions.

Messies are folks of mixed extremes and so find themselves caught in contradictions. When we eliminate the extreme evaluations and come closer to reality, we take a giant step toward reaching our goals. The road is cleared for progress.

It is as we accept, not avoid, ourselves and our houses, acknowledging both weaknesses and strengths, that we can begin to experience the success we desire. Then we'll be winners without playing games.

Write in a sentence something in this chapter that has been meaningful to you.

How can you apply this to your life?

Hello, Hello! Anyone home? Hi, my name is Fred. I am a teacher, a parent, a husband, and an accumulator. Fred's desk—at home or on the job—staggers under the clutter, the disorder, and the debris which accumulates from the multiple responsibilities which are my lot at home and at school.

One of the ironies in all this is that as a consultant or resource person to classroom teachers, one of the most successful and easy-to-make organizers of the classroom is one that I helped design some years ago. I have assisted hundreds of people who sought to organize their desks or the endless array of dittoes lessons, but I have stopped short of trying it myself.

And then there is the YARD SALE approach to clean-up. However, I have such a sense of purpose for virtually all the left-overs from the full-house days or from other households who managed to unload "treasures" for the price of making room that to put a price on each, that is a "quick sale" price, offends my sense of fairness.

As I re-read the above confession, I find myself wondering whether there is a direct relationship between the Messies and the Procrastinators?

Fred / Pennsylvania

Procrastinator's Creed

Knowing that procrastination is, at least in part, a matter of habit, I will do the following as a matter of breaking the procrastination habit:

I will make the bed as soon as it is empty.

I will fill the ice tray immediately and put it away.

I will put the new toilet paper on the roll before it is half used.

I will clear the table, do the dishes, and clean the kitchen immediately after eating. I will consider cleanup a part of the meal.

I will put away what I get out and will not say I will be using it again soon.

I will put away my painting, ceramics, sewing, and other crafts when I am finished for the day, even if I will be using them tomorrow.

I will handle the mail as soon as I pick it up and will not leave it in a pile to consider later.

I will hang up my clothes and put away my shoes as soon as they are off my body.

I will be visually sensitive to anything out of place.

I will remember those three tender little words:

"DO IT NOW"

which my conscience whispers when I am tempted to procrastinate.

95

I found a great method for keeping and clipping coupons, using your box method. I use a four-by-six-inch file box with dividers labeled A-Z and divide my coupons accordingly. For example, shampoo is filed under S, cat food under C, and so on. With the old method of categories, I could never remember if I had filed shampoo under Soaps or Beauty Aids. This saves me time and guesswork and when I'm ready to go shopping, I just bring along my box. It works for me!

Aimee / Washington

9

Messie Burnout

Rediscovering Perspective

Most Messies, I suppose, are garden-variety Messies who live in a disorganized way simply because of personal characteristics that predispose them to it. I was a Messie from the beginning of my marriage when I first attempted to maintain a household, though the house took a while to reach its full bloom of messiness. The point is that disorganization is a natural condition for Messies.

There comes a time when we decide that enough is enough and we want to change. There may be, however, a special complication in the problem of overcoming messiness—the problem of Messie burnout.

People who have Messie burnout are unable to make easy use of the M.A. principles and program. One Messie may read *The New Messie Manual,* put the program in action, and benefit greatly from following the M.A. system. Another Messie may read the same book, feel the same need, try to follow the program, and fall back shortly into her old ways, exhausted because she is burned out. Burned-out Messies try the M.A. program, but it doesn't work for them.

> Burnout is pretty much limited to dynamic, charismatic, goal-oriented men and women . . .

People with the type of personality that makes them Messies are particularly susceptible to the problem of burning out easily. Earlier, I mentioned that Messies tend to be idealists and perfectionists. They are expansive and excessive, giving their all to every project. Being an idealist, the Messie feels her efforts will be rewarded. In his book *Burn-Out* (Bantam Books), Herbert Freidenberger perfectly describes this kind of person:

> Burnout is pretty much limited to dynamic, charismatic, goal-oriented men and women or to determined idealists who want their marriages to be the best, their work records to be outstanding, their children to shine, their community to be better.

Since these characteristics describe the Messie personality so exactly, it is not surprising that we are very susceptible to burnout. It is a problem we must come to grips with. Let's consider first what precipitates burnout in a Messie's life.

Sometimes it is an accumulation of frustrating incidents. Things just slowly become harder and harder to deal with until finally we quit trying to handle them at all. Eventually it doesn't seem important to try anymore because it seems hopeless to continue attempting what we have failed so often at doing. It may be the chronic disorderliness of our husband and kids, the old house without storage space, the constant harping and lack of cooperation of our ever-so-neat spouse, or some vague hidden tedium that wears us down.

Sometimes burnout is triggered by one overpowering incident like:

- a flood that ruined what little order and beauty we had been able to achieve.
- a new baby who tipped the precarious balance into disaster.
- sickness in the family or care of an elderly person.
- a death in the family that leaves us with an "inheritance" we can't deal with—furniture, clothes, pots.
- a move that left us with myriads of boxes and unpacking to do—the final straw.
- any other happening that snows us under to the point where we lose hope of ever tunneling out.

Whether it comes on slowly or quickly, burnout leaves the person feeling powerless and confused.

What is burnout? How can you tell if you have it? The person who is suffering burnout will likely be the last to know because he has lost the sense of perception he needs in order to evaluate what's going on. He is a capable person and feels that with a little more determination and effort he will be able to handle the problem. The problem is that "the hurrieder he goes, the behinder he gets." Effort doesn't produce results. Sometimes, but not always, this is the reason a Messie may work all day and accomplish little.

A person suffering burnout experiences unexplained fatigue, becomes cynical and critical, is unexpectedly sad on occasion, is short-tempered, and has a feeling of disorientation when shifting from one pattern of activities to another (like adjusting to vacation time from work time). He finds himself pulling back from social interaction with friends and family. Sex becomes uninteresting. Routine jobs like writing Christmas cards, making phone calls, filling out forms, and keeping regular appointments are too much to bother with. Eventually he cuts off any activities that seem to be too stressful.

Many people, especially Messies, have some of these characteristics to a degree. If several of the characteristics fit, you need to take care that you aren't beginning to slip into burnout. If so, the earlier it is caught and corrected, the better. However, if you read the list (see "Summary") and say, "Yes! Yes! That's me exactly!" you might want to consider whether you may be suffering a full-blown case of burnout.

I am sure I have gone through some stage of burnout several times in my life. Perhaps you have too. The Messies Anonymous program would not have worked for me if I had tried to put it into practice at any of those times. It will not work for you now if you are burned out.

Sometimes exhaustion, sometimes confusion, sometimes depression were the chief characteristics of the burnout incidents I experienced. (Let me mention that not all burnout is accompanied by depression and not all depression is caused by burnout.) Somehow, I worked through these burnout incidents and came out on the other side, but, I repeat again, I am sure I could not have made any change in the house during the full-blown stage of those incidents even though it was then that the house was at its worst.

Perhaps you can look back and spot a period when you suspect you experienced a burnout incident. Perhaps you suspect you may be having some problems with burnout right now. You must get a handle on this problem in your life before you can begin tackling the house. If you are at the beginning of such a period, you can take steps to put out the flame while it is small before it does more damage to you and the condition of your house.

What can you do about burnout?

The first thought the highly idealistic, hardworking person who is experiencing this type of problem will have is, "I should try harder." This will not work. I am told that if a person is caught in quicksand, the more he tries to get out, the deeper he imbeds himself. It is that way with burnout. More effort and determination will only make things worse.

When more work doesn't do the job, burned-out people seek other help—an excess of drugs (legal or illegal), alcohol, excitement, entertainment such as reading or TV, a profusion of outside activities and distractions. Some of these are perfectly fine in themselves but only harm the burnout when used in excess. In desperation, some hurting burnouts will blank out periods of time, do something really uncharacteristic, and kick over the traces of convention for a wild life.

Since the burned-out person is used to doing everything at full tilt, it is not surprising he overdoes activities in successful areas of his life when he is searching for a way out of his problem.

Many Messies describe to me their incredibly overstuffed lives. They tell various stories.

Work: "I hold two jobs and volunteer at the children's hospital every Thursday."

Family: "I have nine children, all of whom I teach at home except for the two babies, of course."

Fun and culture: "I'm in the little theatre, go to plays and concerts regularly, and take viola lessons twice a week. I'm also working on my masters degree."

Homemaking activities: "I grind my own wheat, bake the bread (whole grain with honey, of course), raise my vegetables, and have my own organically raised chickens—and this is in Manhattan!"

In almost all cases, burning-out Messies feel driven to these tasks to avoid facing their disorganized lives and houses buried under mountains of clutter. Jobs, volunteer work, and hobbies are certainly all desirable and admirable, but not if they are done excessively, for the wrong reasons, and with the wrong approach. After a while, this kind of high-gear lifestyle begins to disintegrate.

We are not omnipotent. But keep this quiet. People in the throes of an activity orgy on the way to burnout think they are—or at least think they ought to be. They are sure the world is totally dependent on them to do their part. What a shock it would be to find that the world could get along quite well if they let up this over-doing. As I have said, it is because many Messies feel so driven and so omnipotent that they seek overactivity as a cure for the distress of burnout. This only makes the house worse.

Again, what can we do about burnout?

We must recognize that we need to make some very specific kinds of changes in our lives so that we are not so mechanical in our approach to life.

"Working," "doing," and "achieving" will have to take a backseat to "being."

You'll remember that in previous chapters I have stressed tuning in to our own feelings and relating to the child within us. This cannot be done as long

102

as a person is interested only in the activities of the world around him.

First you must find a time to be alone—all by yourself. A time alone for yourself alone. It is not easy to find time alone, but if it is important, you can do it.

The second thing you must do is to court and woo the feelings within you. We are so used to thinking we "should" feel a certain way that we hardly know where our true feelings lie.

My aunt, a marvelously gracious hostess, serves soup often as a part of her meals but doesn't take any for herself. Her sister asked her about it.

"I don't really like soup," she said. Surprised, her sister said, "You *used* to like soup!"

"I used to eat it, but I never really liked it," she replied. "Now I don't eat it anymore."

Just at that moment, my own soupspoon halfway to my mouth, I realized I didn't like soup either. Soup makes a nice first course for meals, and people drinking steaming soup on a cold night makes for a cozy scene. Intellectually, I approve of soup, but I really don't like to eat it. For years I ate it because I thought I ought to like it and never admitted my true feelings to myself. It is okay not to like soup.

How many other situations are like that? We think we feel a certain way about something because we have never admitted the truth to ourselves. Most Messies are basically sensitive, artistic people. But when we

> "You do not need to leave your room. Remain sitting at your table and listen. Do not even listen, simply wait. Do not even wait, be quite still and solitary. The world will freely offer itself to you unmasked, it has no choice, it will roll in ecstasy at your feet."
>
> —Franz Kafka

lose touch with our feelings, we are apt to trample our love of order and beauty. When we live in clutter over a period of time, we soon begin to deny to ourselves how much it really bothers us. When we live out of contact with our real selves without knowing it, that causes burnout.

How can we become closer to ourselves? We must pursue that little child within us who is more in touch with our real feelings. This takes time and effort.

It can be done in several ways. Get out your family photo album. Look at it—all alone. Let it prod memories and feelings. Talk to your parents or siblings about the pictures one by one. Seek out the depth of feelings still there but forgotten.

To further stimulate memories, have those who shared your life record their memories for you on a tape recorder.

> "It's real easy to make fun of neatness and of neat people. But if it weren't for us neat people, this world would have gone under a long time ago."
> —Garrison Keillor

Tape record your memories for yourself. This is not a time of deep introspection, but of self-knowledge. Undoubtedly, all memories will not be pleasant. Don't be critical of yourself or others. From the vantage point of an adult, you can approach the past kindly and in a forgiving spirit.

Once you begin to get close to yourself, you can become close to others. It is at these points we begin to find energy and strength. Perhaps we will discover when we know ourselves that we really don't like the way of life we have set up for ourselves and will take steps to make adjustments. Maybe we will find we honestly do like what we are doing and can do it with joy for the first time. We will not be driven to do it with intensity.

It is very important for those coming out of burnout to get help with routine things. The burned-out teacher

104

may hire an older student to help with grading papers. Sometimes our burn-out pivots on one point at which we just stop and cannot cope with certain tasks anymore. If cooking meals becomes too much, buy frozen meals. If you're burned-out with housework, hire someone to come help you—for instance, a boy with a pickup truck to haul away the trash or someone to wash the windows or shampoo the rugs. In short, find someone to help you keep afloat until you are able to take over yourself.

> "Everybody needs his memories. They keep the wolf of insignificance from the door."
> —Saul Bellow

When our lives begin to right themselves from the topsy-turvy mess they are in now, we will be calmer and happier. We will have confidence that our lives are under control. The best thing is that we will then have quality time for ourselves—to read, to think, to plan, to dream. On my key chain I have these words from eighteenth-century poet William Cowper:

> A life all turbulence and noise may seem
> To him that leads it wise and to be praised.
> But wisdom is a pearl with most success
> Sought in still waters.

Summary

Because it is so important for Messies to recognize and handle the burn-out problem, let me summarize what we have covered.

- Many Messies experience burnout in the area of housekeeping because of the stress of chronic disorganization.

- We seek relief from housekeeping burnout by seeking more activities outside of the home. We become driven doers.

- In order to overcome burnout, we need to cut back on our activities and seek out our own personal feelings. Only then will we begin to pull out of this debilitating experience.

- While in the burn-out phase, we need to seek outside help for some of the activities we find we are unable to do.

- We need to recognize that burnout does not have to be permanent. If we handle it with understanding, we will be able to face our responsibilities with enthusiasm and success.

1. Are there any periods in your life when you experienced burnout and were unable to perform the basics of housekeeping? Identify the occasions and what it was that seemed to precipitate the burnout.
   a. Occasion
      Cause
   b. Occasion
      Cause

2. Is there any important activity you have ceased to do because it has become "just too much"? If so, name it.

   Who can you get to do this activity for you for a while? (If you don't know a person by name, put down the kind of person you will keep your eye out for.)

3. If you could have an afternoon or day totally to yourself for fun, what three activities might you do?

   a.

   b.

   c.

4. When was the last time you did any of these? Put that date next to each activity above.

I am having a ball cleaning out everything. I told my husband, "If I don't need it, I'm getting rid of it." Immediately he changed a burnt-out light bulb in the kitchen and a burnt-out headlight on the car. I guess he thought I meant him, too.

Carla / Ohio

part 4

Nuts and Bolts
for Messies

10

Actually Cleaning the House

Let us assume that your house has come under a moderate degree of organizational control. If it hasn't, there's not much reason to talk about cleaning. In the first place, cleaning is not all that rewarding in a cluttered house. It doesn't look or feel that much improved after you finish. Clean clutter doesn't have much advantage over dirty clutter. In the second place, cleaning is too hard to do when you've already been defeated just trying to hold on to some semblance of order. All the clutter will prove too much of a hindrance in doing the job.

Messies frequently say their houses are clean, even if they are cluttered. Messies generally have a high regard for cleanliness and healthful living. We may let the dishes go unwashed until germs multiply, but when we do wash

111

them, we scald them or rinse them in disinfectant. However, because it is so difficult to really clean a cluttered house, the house is probably not as clean as a Messie believes it is. I'm not talking bubonic plague here. I'm just saying that a messy house is almost impossible to clean well or consistently. However, once the house is reasonably orderly, we can get around to actually cleaning it.

A straightforward approach to cleaning dirt will go a long way, so let's consider the cleaning task before us. The dirty stuff we want to get rid of comes in three forms:

1. the big stuff like tennis shoes and deodorant bottles,
2. the little stuff like dust and dirt, and
3. the congealed stuff you find around the bathtub, in the kitchen, and on the baseboards.

We attack them in that order.

But before the attack begins, we need to retreat for a few minutes and take a detour to the Mount Vernon Method—what I've come to refer to as a Messie's Declaration of Independence.

Some years ago during my desperate search for help, a Cleanie friend told me about the Mount Vernon Method. While touring George Washington's estate, my friend had been so impressed with the maintenance that she made a point of asking the woman who was in charge of housekeeping about the method they used.

The housekeeper explained that she directs her cleaners to start at the front door and work their way around the outside periphery of the room. When one room is finished, they proceed to the next, doing everything that needs to be done in each room so the rooms are left clean and organized. They dust and wax from the time they come to work early in the day until it is time

112

for the public to arrive. A few minutes before opening time, the workers collect their boxes of cleaning supplies and leave. Each day they begin where they left off the day before and keep going from room to room until it is quitting time.

But it is easy to clean Mount Vernon. George is not there to mess it up! I decided not to use the method for dusting and polishing, for cleaning walls, drapes, upholstery, or carpets. First I needed to get organized. I started at the front door.

The first item of furniture beside my front door was a lamp table with one small drawer. After I had cleaned out that little drawer, throwing away several very old school calendars, old classified ads, and a lot of junk, I felt I could do anything.

Next, I came to a piece of living room furniture with six drawers, two of which literally had not been opened for years. I was actually afraid to open them. Why afraid? I think I believed I would not be able to handle what I found—that my decision-making apparatus would be sprung and broken.

"I can honestly say that we have never missed anything that we got rid of. We did replace one ancient single bed which we sold and later needed. Cost was seventy-five dollars—a small price for the use of a room for three years. (The bedroom had been so stuffed with junk, it was unused until then!)"

But after a good night's rest, I did open the drawers. The challenge turned out to be a paper tiger. I could easily handle the things I found there. There were no terrible decisions to make. I am still surprised at the unreasonable fear I felt about those drawers.

As I continued around the house I threw out twelve-year-old medicine from my medicine cabinet. In my clothes closet I came across my wedding shoes. They were twenty-three years old, were missing a decorative buckle, and had never fit. However, I thought perhaps someday I might locate the buckle, and they might come back in style. (You never can tell, you know. Miracles *do* happen!)

I threw them out. I wasn't going to let the past with its lovely memories muddle today. Messies must learn to live with their hopeless sentimentality.

The most important thing about the Mount Vernon Method is to pace yourself and not overdo. You will not be able to accomplish the Method in a single day (it took me three-and-a-half months to "Mount Vernonize" my home).

Think of this as a marathon as opposed to a sprint. A sprint is a short-term race and requires maximum energy output right from the beginning. Housekeeping is a marathon, not a sprint. Go slow and steady because you don't want to wear yourself out. Don't start a whole closet if it is too much. Plan to do two shelves at a time if you can handle this better.

When you have done enough for one day, stop. Wait until the next day. Take one day off each week so you can look forward to a break. I also advise that you leave the kitchen until last. Kitchens aren't for rookies!

Don't save a matchbook for Mary's son who saves matchbooks.

When you are ready to start, make a list of several items—three to seven—that you plan to do each day before you start Mount Vernonizing. Remember that the Mount Vernon Method is for organizing, not for heavy cleaning.

Begin at the front door and start with the first piece of furniture you come to that has a nook, cranny, drawer, or whatever. As you move from one spot to another, take with you three boxes: a give-away box, a throw-away box, and a storage box. Open the first drawer.

114

Throw away every piece of junk that has accumulated there. Be serious about it. Don't keep the pen that works only half the time; toss the pretty calendar that's more than a year old. Your freedom from clutter is more important than they are.

When you find things that are too good to throw out, put them in the give-away box. And give them away quickly! You'll be glad you shared. Two cautions are in order:

1. Don't take anything out of the give-away box once you've put it in (unless it is really important to you to do so.)
2. Don't wait for the perfect time or the perfect person to give it to. Get rid of it right away. Don't save a matchbook for Mary's son who saves matchbooks. Don't even save it for a garage sale unless you have a specific date set for a sale. After that date, give it to the closest charity.

Be willing to take a risk that you may later want what you discarded. Remember that although it may cause temporary pain to throw something out, it causes definite pain to keep it. Tossing it out is mild pain compared with the pain that comes from having to live helplessly with all that clutter. There is an exhilarating feeling of freedom that comes once the decision is made to take control of the house.

"Every day I'll throw something away, and I'll soon feel better and better."

—Motto, Pack Rats
Anonymous
Peg Bracken

The storage box is there to keep the things that don't need to be discarded but are in the wrong place. Do not hop up and put them in another place while you are cleaning because this will break your concentration. You may never return to your job there. Just put

115

them into the box to be put away when you finally reach the place where each belongs.

It does not matter how quickly you complete the Mount Vernon phase. What matters is that you are consistent in your efforts and determination to complete the task.

Now, with that important bit of knowledge under our belts, let's return to our actual cleaning.

First, remove any of those big items that have crept out from where you put them now that you've Mount Vernonized the house. Being distractible and forgetful—and living with others who may be, too—these faux pas will occur. Shuttle them back to their places or have the perpetrators do it. If these items don't have a place to be put, this is your signal to

a. get rid of more unnecessary stuff because it is taking up important space,
b. get some more storage helps such as shelves,
c. rethink the system of storage you have set up, or
d. all of the above.

Once the big stuff is removed, we think about the little stuff such as dust and tracked-in dirt. A dust removal spray product on a soft cloth wiped over surfaces (both horizontal *and* vertical) does a great job. Variations on this system include using spray wax instead. This leaves a nice, temporary smell in the house. As far as I can tell, spray wax does not leave uncontrollable "waxy build-up." Use only one brand of polish once you start because sometimes different wax sprays don't mix well, and the combination turns milky. You can use a lamb's wool duster if you like. It has the advantage of attracting dust (so they say) to it, and it approaches the magic wand many Messies would like to find to clean

Ten Commandments of Housekeeping

I. Thou shalt not try to do everything thyself.
Get help from children, husband, and hired
cleaners as you can.

II. Thou shalt have a goal,
for without a goal, nothing will be accomplished.

III. Thou shalt have a plan and stick to it.

IV. Remember the family to treat them in love
while you (and they) are changing.

V. Thou shalt not overschedule
and thus shalt not say "yes" to everyone who asks.
Set your own priorities and say "yes" or "no" in line
with them. Take control of your activities.

VI. Thou shalt dream and keep dreaming until your
lifestyle fits the dream.

VII. Thou shalt reward thyself for jobs well done and
milestones met.

VIII. Thou shalt make housework easy to do by
organizing for efficiency, because only as work is
easily done will we do much of it.

IX. Thou shalt find joy in beauty and order.
We are not accomplishing these goals only for
utilitarian purposes. Only as we take joy in our
accomplishments will we be willing to continue.

X. Thou shalt not procrastinate.
Keep things up and do jobs as soon as thou shalt
notice they need doing. Do not leave it out to be put
away later.

the house anyway. It is also fast and will reach higher
spots. The disadvantage is that I suspect not all the dust
is being magnetically attracted—it will hang in the air
just long enough to fool us and fall back down as soon
as we turn our backs. Feather dusters, by the way, do
very little but rearrange dust, so avoid them. Keep your

eyes open in the store and commercials for new and "exciting" dusting products.

Messies don't dust as often as other people because they like to actually see the dust before they tackle it. Some other folks dust regularly whether they can see it or not, on the premise that it must be there building up secretly. They nip it in the bud. We let it develop a little.

Next, vacuum to get rid of any dust that got knocked onto the floor when you dusted and to pick up any dirt tracked in. Try to bring yourself to vacuum the furniture occasionally. Here you must take it on faith that the dust you see on the tables is also getting on the couch and chairs. No magic shield covers upholstery. If you don't vacuum it off, it somehow attacks the fibers and rots them away. There are several mysteries about dirt that remain unexplained. How and why dust ruins fiber is one of them. But the fact remains that, explained or not, it does. Eventually, if the dust and dirt are not periodically removed, our furniture looks prematurely old. Vacuuming the upholstered furniture is like flossing teeth—it does more good in the long run than it seems to be doing at the time you do it.

Thou shalt find joy in beauty and order.

At this point, we hit the second mystery about dirt— cobwebs. Why some dirt hangs in strings from the ceiling is beyond me. A man who had a doctorate in physics told me that he had no idea what made cobwebs. Since that time, I have pondered the subject with little success. What *is* clear, however, is that cobwebs come down easily if you sweep them down using a broom sprayed with a dust removal product or a broom wrapped with a dust cloth or a lamb's wool duster which doesn't streak the ceiling.

Third, we come to the grimy part—how to destroy the dirt that clings. This step involves a lot of decision

118

making since this is the kind of dirt that needs to be attacked with cleaning products. The number of cleaning products available is wonderfully overwhelming. The choices are myriad. Here Messies run into problems about what to use where.

"Nothing in excess."

—Euripides

On more than one occasion, I have had bad experiences using products that were too strong. One ate the indicator numbers off my stove knobs. Once my daughter used a tile cleaner on the tub and removed all the glaze. The tub will never be the same. Powdered cleansers will do the same thing to a tub or sink if used long enough, all except one product which has a chicken on it and claims it hasn't scratched anything yet. To top it all off, I once mixed bleach and ammonia. This produces a poisonous gas that can cause death or injury. The possibilities for making cleaning mistakes are many, and Messies hate mistakes. So Messies are inclined to avoid cleaning.

Time Saver

Basic Cleaning Supplies

Kitchen	General	Bathrooms
sponges (with and without scrubber backing)	vacuum cleaner with attachments	sponge
	dustcloths	liquid cleanser with bleach
dish detergent	window squeegee	toilet bowl brush
dishwasher detergent	bucket	small garbage bags
garbage bags	sponges	ammonia
steel-wool pads	trash bags	old toothbrush
cleanser	small tool kit	tile cleaner
paper towels	broom	
old toothbrush	dust mop	
	sponge mop	
	dustpan	
	window cleaner	

119

How does a person know what to use? I am not going to recommend that you mix your own or go to commercial cleaning supply houses. These may be good ideas on rare occasions, but for Messies, the easier products are to get and to use, the more likely it is that we'll do the job. How can you tell which products will do the kind of job you want?

Boring as it may seem, it is a good idea to read the labels on the boxes. These people want their products to sell so they tell you where to use them and how to make them most effective.

Clothes-washing detergents are geared to different needs. Some clean grease; some clean protein stains like those from grass and blood. Some leave good smells. Some soften. Some are general. Most are probably pretty much the same with a few changes.

Automatic dishwasher detergents tell you to use water at 140 degrees. If the water's not hot enough, the soap won't dissolve. It will gum up your dishwasher and cause leakage. This will rot your cabinets and floor. Sadness will occur as your disaster spreads.

Every once in a while a problem develops that you really have trouble with and nothing you can find seems to work. I had that trouble recently with the colored ink from a bread bag. The print left bright stains on my light-colored Formica kitchen counter. Nothing removed it until I used my liquid dishwasher detergent. It whisked it away like a miracle.

I realize that this product has some chlorine bleach in it, and bleach is not recommended for Formica. Some other product may exist that will do better. I don't know of any offhand. Sometimes you have to make compromises for necessities.

Now we come to the third and last mystery about dirt. As dirt sits, it begins to evolve into gunk. Gunk needs to be rubbed off. Nice, gentle dust that floats softly down onto the baseboards will turn into tough, angry grime if left indefinitely. An easy-flowing liquid stain will become a permanent blot if left too long. I believe that dirt and stains have little hands so they can grope for other dirt particles. They all clench their fists tightly together and grab each other and whatever they touch. They clench tighter day by day until you have to use dynamite to blast them apart. Get the little rascals off as soon as you can, before their nasty little hands clench too tightly. One secret you need to know is that the right cleaning product, if left to soak for a short time, will soften the hardest gunk like magic. No dynamite necessary!

> "We know what a man thinks not when he tells us what he thinks, but by his actions."
>
> —Isaac Bashevis Singer

What are the "right" cleaning products? Books could be written about cleaning methods and products. As a matter of fact, several have been.

The original Mr. Clean, Don Aslett, writes books regularly on how to streamline cleaning techniques. Being a professional cleaner, he recommends professional products. This has an alluring appeal to perfectionist Messies. Let's make an agreement. Start out using regular, supermarket-type household products until your house begins to come round. Then switch over to professional products a little at a time if you must.

> If there's something you don't do, hate to do, and feel guilty about not doing, get help.

Check out your local book store and flip through the books you find there dealing with the subject of cleaning. Or search through your Internet bookstore offerings and see what books are recommended.

Finally, we speak of the windows. Bright, shiny windows add a special charm to houses. If you have many windows, you will wear yourself out using the spritz-bottle-and-paper-towel routine. Instead, use the professional window cleaner's method. Water with ammonia in it and a small dash of Joy dishwashing liquid applied with a sponge and wiped off with the kind of window squeegees used on car windshields will make the windows shiny bright in no time. Well, *no time* is a bit of an exaggeration, but it will be less time and effort than it would be otherwise.

> "What can be done at any time, is never done at all."
>
> —English Proverb

For the hard stuff, get outside help. Maids in the old-fashioned sense are a thing of the past. Cleaning services and cleaning people—there's where the help is today. If there's something you don't do, hate to do, and feel guilty about not doing, get help.

Let's take one step back before we leave this subject. In general, cleaning is *not* the problem Messies face. It's important and it has a place, but the big problem for Messies is household control.

What's keeping *you* from getting around to cleaning the house? Check any factors you feel may apply to you.

__I lose the cleaning products.

__It's unfair—my family should help more.

__It's just not important to me. I have better uses for my time.

__I'm uncertain about how to do it.

__I'm uncertain about which products are best.

__Cleaning products cost too much.

__I don't have the right equipment (mops, sponges, vacuum cleaner, etc.).

__Other:

What changes would make cleaning easier for you?

1.
2.
3.
4.
5.
6.
7.
8.
9.
10.
11.
12.
13.
14.
15.

Special Prayers for Messies
(with special thanks to Claudia)

A Prayer for the Kitchen

God grant me the energy to tackle this mess, the wisdom to face it, and the courage to not set off dynamite.

A Prayer for the Bathroom

God help me to tear the seal off the can of Comet, the wisdom to use the plunger, and the courage (yes, the courage) to even shake the cleanser can into the proper places.

A Prayer for the Family Room

God, if it pleases Thee, help me not to set a match to this room. (The children really do love their dog.)

A Prayer for the Living Room

God, You know I am weak. I make attempts to keep this room junk-free, but help me not to wallow in too much self-pride!

A Prayer for My Refrigerator Drawers

Please help, God, this limp celery, to revive itself. After all, the starving children in India would eat this gladly.

A Prayer for the Bedroom

Oh closet doors, please keepest thou closed, or else when thou openest, the junk inside wilst fall and break my nose.

A Prayer for the Twelve-Year-Old's Room

When, dear God, as I look on the mounds of clothing, the dried Sugar Daddy in the corner, and the half-taped motorcycle poster on the wall, will I get more than a low grunt from Waldo, Jr., when I say, "Clean this room or you die at daybreak"? Will he ever stop saying, "I didn't do it. It's not my fault"?

A Prayer for the Garage

Oh slime of oil oozing through the cracks of cement, please hide thou under my car until I can Mount Vernonize my house. Then you are next!

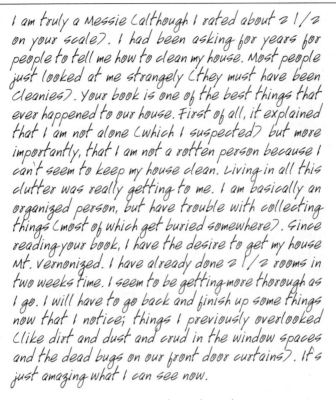

I am truly a Messie (although I rated about 2 1/2
on your scale). I had been asking for years for
people to tell me how to clean my house. Most people
just looked at me strangely (they must have been
Cleanies). Your book is one of the best things that
ever happened to our house. First of all, it explained
that I am not alone (which I suspected) but more
importantly, that I am not a rotten person because I
can't seem to keep my house clean. Living in all this
clutter was really getting to me. I am basically an
organized person, but have trouble with collecting
things (most of which get buried somewhere). Since
reading your book, I have the desire to get my house
Mt. Vernonized. I have already done 2 1/2 rooms in
two weeks time. I seem to be getting more thorough as
I go. I will have to go back and finish up some things
now that I notice; things I previously overlooked
(like dirt and dust and crud in the window spaces
and the dead bugs on our front door curtains). It's
just amazing what I can see now.

The dream of being able to get control of my house
is one I had given up on. Thank you for all the time
and effort you put into writing this book. The dream
of having time to do things is another one I had
practically given up on. Now I have a happier future.
Only another Messie could understand this.

Carol / Wisconsin

Things I Did When Sanity Began to Return

Messies are terribly patient people—emphasize *terribly*. We put up with insults to our dignity from a house that few people would spend more than ten minutes in. We have endured an uncomfortable way of living for so long that we tune out the discomfort it causes us. Like a rock in our shoe, we don't realize how much it hurts until we get rid of it.

The purpose of this chapter is to tune us in to the little rocks that hurt.

As I was getting used to the Mount Vernon Method, wisps of organizational sanity began to drift through the windmills of my mind. I noticed that although the house was definitely clearing up as I got rid of the junk, I did not know what to do with the things I chose to keep. I began to be dissatisfied with the just-pile-them-anywhere approach.

> The house began to clear out and my mind began to clear up.

The house began to clear out, and my mind began to clear up. I noticed several needs I had overlooked before. I'll mention the areas I found in my house as examples. As you think of your own particular needs in your house, jot them down in the margin to use later in the question part of the chapter.

Bathroom Clutter

When soap, shampoo, conditioners, tissues, and so on find their resting place on the bathroom windowsill and across the back of the toilet, the place always looks unkempt and is impossible to clean. I got rid of a bunch of creams, powders, and bubble baths I never used and put the rest of the things on a shower caddy which had a holder for washcloths built in.

By the way, I quit saving slivers of soap. I do not compress them together for future use. I do not squeeze them into a liquid-soap dispenser with water to substitute for liquid soap. I do not put them into a pocket in a sponge for a bathing experience. When a new bar of soap comes in, slivers slither into the trash can. The few pennies saved are not worth the aggravation. Now I have a bar of soap for the tub and a liquid-soap dispenser for the sink. The windowsill is completely clear, and one box of tissues is the only thing on the back of the toilet. Makes wipe-up easy, and it looks great.

Bare is beautiful—at least in the bathroom. Life was beginning to get easier and more pleasant.

Linen Closet

In the linen closet, I divided everything into groups (curtains, hooks, etc.) and put them into clear plastic shoe boxes. I labeled each box and stacked them on the shelves, three-deep.

The pillowcases I put in a square plastic dishpan *and* labeled it with a file-folder label so I could easily know what was in there without having to check. I did the same with curtains. Sheets I put in a larger, milk-carton-type of holder sold in the organizations sections of many stores.

I also bought a wall-mounted holder to keep the iron and its cord out of the way. I put up cup hooks for the flyswatter and curling iron. I got a broom holder attachment for the wall to get the broom off the floor.

Christmas Decorations

Christmas decorations varied in my house from year to year because one year I would find one box of decorations I had stored, and the next year I would find another box with a different assortment of decorations. We had three Christmas tree stands scattered around in storage that we bought when the ones we had did not come out of hiding in time for Christmas.

That was before I found a Christmas tree storage box specially made to store Christmas things. It is large and red and has pictures of Christmas ornaments on it. It is not easy to lose. All of the Christmas decorations are in its specially constructed compartments. The door wreath and resident tree stand are beside it on the upper closet shelf. Come on Christmas! We're ready for you now.

Shoes

I had a wire shoe holder, but I did not really have the patience to lean over into the closet and deposit each shoe in its place. Besides, I had more shoes than holders, and the extras just lay on top of those shoes that were on holders. The open bottom collected dust like mad. Solution: chuck the shoe holder and get a lovely beige-and-blue corrugated cardboard holder that wouldn't get dust under it and on top of which extra shoes could sit nicely in their boxes. I didn't have to lean into the back of the closet to wrestle the shoes onto holders. I also got a matching shelf organizer for purses.

Friends, life was beginning to improve. Little things mean a lot.

Jewelry

My high school jewelry box was much too little to hold what needed to get into it. I had had it for twenty-five years, so it was sentimental to me. I was not used to spending money on organizational things, so the price of a larger jewelry box seemed like too much. Instead, I asked for and got a large jewelry box from my husband for Christmas. One storage problem solved.

Night Clothes

Up until this time, I had kept my nightgown and robe on little hooks in the back of the closet, which was a nuisance because there weren't enough hooks. I had to wade through clothes on hangers to get back there to hang them up and get them out. The hooks were so small the night clothes fell off into a heap on the floor. Sometimes I gave up and just put them on the foot of the bed.

129

Hat rack to the rescue. On the back of the door of the bathroom that adjoins my bedroom, I hung a plastic hat rack. It had ten or so large knobs, enough to hang plenty of clothes easily and securely. What an improvement.

Plug Outlets

There was a spot where I needed three outlets and had only two. I kept having to plug and unplug, plug and unplug—a needless aggravation. I bought a four-pronged outlet which works great.

Assorted Improvements

On and on it went. As I continued with the Mount Vernon Method, I began to see place after place where I had allowed myself to be frustrated simply because I had not made plans to solve chronic problems.

Knife holder. Knives stored in drawers chip each other and are hard to get to. I bought a magnetic knife holder to store knives by the stove.

Pot holders. Pot holders must have some place to be stored or else they lie on the counter collecting food stains. This had been where mine stayed while waiting to be used. I put up three cup hooks and hung my decorative pot holders on them like pictures.

Can opener. The can opener cutter wheel was worn down. Opening a can was an "iffy" proposition. It left unopened gaps. We went around the half-opened lid again and again—each time becoming more and more frustrated. When I finally tuned in to the trouble I was putting up with, I replaced it. By the way, while I was at it, I got rid of the melon baller and its never-used relatives.

130

Personal tools. I don't know whether the men in my family can keep up with their tools or not, but I know I can't. I got tired of needing a tool and not being able to find one, so I bought my own set of screwdrivers at a great sale at a local variety store. I keep them in my personal dresser drawer and now I always have the tools I need. This is an example of creative problem solving in action.

Don't sweat the little things. It will take a little time to get used to having a non-Messie home.

On and on it went. I got two clothes hampers, a light-colored one for light clothes and a dark-colored one for dark clothes. This streamlined sorting. I got a round belt holder so I wouldn't have to look for belts hither, thither, and yon. I hung my tablecloths on a staggered shirt hanging system.

I didn't notice or correct these problems all at once. It took time.

The point is that once you become sensitive to all of the spots in the house where you are continually experiencing frustration, you can begin to take the rocks out of your shoe one by one and, oh, does it feel good!

1. Are there any painful rocks in your bedroom? What might be a solution for each one?

ROCK   Solution

_____   _____

_____   _____

_____   _____

2. Are there any rocks in the bathroom?

ROCK   Solution

_____   _____

_____   _____

_____   _____

3. Are there any rocks in the kitchen?

ROCK   Solution

_____   _____

_____   _____

_____   _____

4. Are there any rocks in the kids' rooms?

ROCK   Solution

_____   _____

_____   _____

_____   _____

5. Are there any rocks in the den (playroom, study)?

ROCK   Solution

_____   _____

_____   _____

_____   _____

6. Are there any rocks in the basement?

ROCK   Solution

_____   _____

_____   _____

_____   _____

7. Are there any rocks in the garage?

ROCK   Solution

_____   _____

_____   _____

_____   _____

8. Are there any rocks in the attic?

ROCK   Solution

_____   _____

_____   _____

_____   _____

9. Are there any other areas of frustration you may not have listed yet? What about solutions for these?

ROCK   Solution

_____   _____

_____   _____

_____   _____

I am so happy I'm getting a second chance to write to you. I read about you in the Sun Times. I cut out the article and wanted to join M.A. Unfortunately, the article got lost in my clutter. I'm going to put this letter in my car so it doesn't get lost in my cluttered house.

I really need your help. I'm a very neat person at heart. I love and appreciate neatness. I envy neatness. Why is my house such a mess?

You were talking about me when you mentioned piles. It seems whenever I clean one room, the adjacent room gets everything from the room I've cleaned. It's a vicious circle and I can't stand it.

I don't appreciate my husband's snide remarks about the way I "clean"—moving piles around from room to

133

room. But of course he's right. He's even offered to get me a cleaning-lady. I haven't been able to organize the house to the point where I could have someone come in and clean it.

I'd like to read the books you've written, I need all the help you can offer. I'm sorry I don't have your name. I wrote it on another piece of paper and can't find it.

Help! Help! Help!—as fast as you can.

Estelle / Illinois

12

If You Want to Dance, You Have to Pay the Piper

My friend was an undeclared Messie. She had a vague, nagging feeling that her house was unpleasant to be in. She really admired the lovely houses her grandchildren had but felt it must be because they had more decorating sense than she did.

Exercise equipment was in her living room along with two sofas, three chairs, and too many tables. A Mother's Day plate sat on the kitchen counter along with mail trays, decorative pictures, and piles of coupons. And yet she was neat and organized in her own way. The news clippings were all in one pile where she could find them, the books were all shelved and some shelves were covered over with plastic to protect the books, the magazine piles were all on the coffee table. She had two large closets of clothes and two bathrooms of powders, salves, ointments, creams, antiseptics, and what-have-you. She could always find what she wanted.

"My house is such a mess," she said. "I just don't like going home anymore."

"What would you do to improve your house if you could?" I asked.

"Well, the sofa needs replacing. I've had it so long, and it looks drab. My floor is so hard to keep nice. It needs to be covered with some kind of tile to make it nicer." The truth is that if both the sofa and the floor were replaced, they would look nicer, but the house would still look the same.

> Until the clutter that dams up the house is removed, beauty cannot flow in.

I can understand her approach exactly. When my house was in a dither, I could hardly figure out where the problem was either. I thought I needed an interior decorator, but I didn't know what I would say to one. Messies' houses *are* unpleasant, but the problem is not with the decorations. Until the clutter that dams up the house is removed, beauty cannot flow in, no matter how many sofas you replace.

Having said this, there is another side to the story. When I finally began to clear away the clutter in my house and mind, I noticed a remarkable thing—my house really *was* ugly.

The walls were green, the indoor-outdoor carpet was aqua, the dining room chairs were upholstered in burgundy, and, to top it all off, we had orange accent pieces since my husband's favorite color was orange. The funny part was I had given careful consideration to each choice, and it hadn't worked out very well at all. I had two sofas, a vinyl recliner, and a homemade dresser with one drawer bottom falling out (but you didn't notice it unless you opened the drawer). There were some end tables and a stereo too. The stereo didn't work. The lamps were becoming dingy with age. Friends, we are talking mega-ugly here, but before the clutter cleared, I didn't realize how ugly it was. My house begged for beauty. It was slow, but sure, in coming. But there were obstacles.

Messies, being frugal and creative, are slow to spend money on the house. I considered painting the hand-made dresser (and actually bought an antiquing kit) or covering it with Chinese newspapers for interest and varnishing the whole thing, but I never could find Chinese newspapers. I wrote to the lamp company to complain about the lamps. They wrote back saying they were sorry.

You can't make a silk purse out of a sow's ear. I had the sow's ear, but silk purses cost money. My big mental breakthrough came when I was finally willing to spend money on the house. Over the six years since I first began to change, I have made replacements—doing thoughtful comparison shopping and slowly making careful choices since my tastes are obviously not finely tuned.

For Christmas I asked for and got a breakfront for the china—out went the homemade dresser. The two sofas, so useful for sleeping overnight guests, were banished in favor of a beautiful hide-a-bed sofa. The aqua indoor-outdoor rug was replaced with mauve wall-to-wall carpeting. The kitchen and dining room floors were tiles in a matching pink, gray, and beige marblelike tile with coordinated grout. We painted the walls beige. I won't bother you with more details except to say that it looks so lovely now.

But what about the money? It takes a lot of money to do all of this.

I had always marveled at the nice-looking houses of families who seemed to be in our income bracket. Where did they get the money?

First of all, beauty was important to them, so they were willing to put out for it. Messies might readily spend $12.95 for a book or some craft item but resist spending it on something to spruce up the house. People-oriented expenditures (private school, camp, vacations, phone calls) or intellectual, cultural, and creative pursuits, such as plays, extension courses at college, books, music CDs, and art or music supplies have priority with Messies. Wooden pieces of furniture seem so temporal. Why get a new sofa if the old one is still useful? My neighbors put a priority on a beautiful house, and even though I thought I did, I didn't.

The second reason they are able to have lovely houses is because of what I call magnetic goal setting. Once a person really sets a goal to have a beautiful house, she will attract the ideas, the money, and even the actual furnishings she needs. It is not a supernatural thing; it is simply the natural way thoughts work. It is not mysterious once you know why and how it works, but it is amazing to see it happen. Suffice it to say here that once you set out in search of beauty, you will see bargains you would have overlooked before, friends will cooperate to help you locate what you are looking for, you will find extra money you would have frittered away before, and you will discover your tastes beginning to develop. You will begin to notice unique ways of creating beauty.

In my case, a marvelous carpenter friend had a week off and volunteered to help us put down the tile floor. By the end of the week he had painted the ceiling and walls of the living room, dining room, and kitchen as well and bought all the supplies at a discount. (Thanks again, Mike. No one else could have done it as well!) The sofa and carpet were both on sale. The kitchen cabinets, which I haven't mentioned, we got at a factory outlet. The beige lace tablecloth I put over the pink solid cloth on the dining room table was bought at an after-Christmas sale.

There were slipups and mistakes, of course, and I don't pretend to be a supercareful shopper. I don't have time for it. I don't have stylish taste, and what taste I have doesn't come easily. If you know what you want, however, you stumble across it more often than you would imagine. It takes time, but it happens. If it could work for me, it can work for anybody.

> Once you set out in search of beauty, you will see bargains you would have overlooked before.

If money were no object, list three—and only three—areas of improvement that would require major expenditures at your house (apartment, room, or whatever).

_____

_____

_____

Put *A* beside the one that would make the most significant positive change in the house, *B* beside the next most important, and *C* beside the third most important in terms of positive significance. List the cost on the three lines to the right of each.

Put a star beside the one you feel will be most within your power to change.

I have discovered that baskets can make a big difference on laundry day. I have a different color basket for every member of our family, and as I sort and fold clean laundry, I put the clean clothes in the

proper basket. It is so much easier for the kids to manage. I find that I can use the baskets for all those things they may leave around the house. My next goal is to teach the kids to do the laundry!

Cindy / Indiana

13

More Dancing, More Pipers, More Payment

Not far from the university library where I now sit writing is a duck named Joseph. He lives on a small lake that is a part of this park-like tropical campus in south Florida. The lake is not very wide, but it is long. Joseph is fat, fed from the lunch bags of the students who eat around the lake. Ducks, especially fat ducks, are awkward on land, efficient on water. And yet Joseph will not swim. Day after day he laboriously walks the long distance around the lake rather than swim the short distance across it. Joseph actually is able to swim. Once, in desperation, after a long weekend without scraps of lunches, he swam across for a bread handout. On the whole, however, he chooses the slow, hard way of navigation while the other ducks on the lake swim.

Why Joseph chooses to operate this way I do not know any more than I know why I and other Messies choose the hard way of living when easier ways are available.

Begin to think of ways you can make life easier for yourself. As you read, make notes in the margin about your ideas for your house. In the last chapter, I mentioned several changes I made. In this chapter, I will mention several more that might stimulate your thinking about your situation.

Help for a Small House

Florida houses are small. Most have no basement or attic and in many cases, no garage. Though my house was sturdily made to stand up to hurricanes, it had very little storage room. For years, even after I had turned the corner on messiness, I was, like Joseph the duck, unwilling to face the facts about how hard things were for me because I lacked storage area. I kept trying to live in an overcrowded house (my husband and I both use our house for an office) by packing things in closer, tighter, and more efficiently. Finally, I faced facts and got a ten-by-ten shed. It was absolutely necessary if I were going to stop clunking around the lake the hard way and start swimming efficiently in my house.

Telephone Area

The telephone area in our house just wasn't working out. My husband took messages at the dining room table, on the backs of envelopes, and on scraps of paper. Usually they were misplaced or put in a pile on the dining room windowsill (an unsightly array that fell off whenever the curtain was opened or closed). Like Joseph, we kept doing it the hard way.

How long it was before I got the telephone answering pad, I don't know. I *highly* recommend it for you to solve the phone message problem.

The book I have is eleven-by-six inches. It has four perforated easy-to-tear-out areas on each page. That way, when you take a phone message you'll need to give to someone, you can tear it out easily.

To make it more efficient, when you write on a page it makes a carbonless permanent duplicate on the yellow page below it. Here's how it works. Let's say I receive a message for my son from a college asking for a list of things he must have his high school send to the admissions office. I write down the list, tear out the information, and give it to my son as a reminder for him to take to school. He loses the paper. Never fear! I have a permanent duplicate of that message on my yellow permanent pad. It is amazing how many times I refer to the telephone answering pad for a reminder.

The telephone books were problems too. Our main phone area is in the dining room next to the kitchen. Miami has three huge books, and we are also blessed with smaller family directories from church and school. We kept them in the hall closet some distance from the phone. It was a real nuisance. I needed a place for my answering pad as well. The phone was close to the kitchen, but there was no drawer there for all these books. In line with the Messie principles, I set a goal for a telephone table and, sure enough, not long after I saw just the right thing in a catalog and sent for it.

Needless to say, you need to keep a pen with your telephone message pad—preferably a ball-point pen, which will make enough impression to mark through to that yellow copy page. If people keep stealing it from the phone table, tie it to the table or the phone. There

143

are pens at office supply stores with attachments for that very purpose.

Time Saver

Telephone Time

Use the latest technology for efficiency and ease. Things are changing fast. Today's new gadget is quickly replaced. You have many choices to have a telephone close to you so you can use it conveniently, sometimes on your belt, in an ear plug, or whatever so you can do many other things while you talk.

On the other hand, maybe you don't want to be disturbed by telephone conversations. There are answering machines, voice mail, and caller ID to shield you from unwanted interruptions. When you return calls, you are the caller and more in control of the timing of the call, when to place it and when to hang up.

The One-Minute Messie No Empty Arms

Make a promise to yourself that you will not enter or leave a room in your house without improving its appearance. Just putting a toy or book away or straightening the towels in the bathroom will make the room look better. Better yet, keep dustcloths (some specially treated to attract dust or for polishing in pop-out dispensers) in handy, out-of-the-way places, and by the time you've gone in and out of a room a few times, you may have it dusted! Use handy treated cleaning cloths to improve kitchen and bathrooms.

Make every trip count. Every time you go upstairs, take something along that needs to be taken up. Same with trips to the basement, garage, from the car, from

144

the office. Look around before you go, and don't go empty-handed.

File Area

In my book *The New Messies Manual* I say a few succinct words about filing and won't say much more here except as it bears on spending money.

You need a filing cabinet—a two-drawer file is best, but you may have to move up to a four-drawer cabinet if you really need it.

You need hanging-file holders—Pendaflex™ is a good brand found along with others in office supply stores. Others will do and are found in most general product or variety stores.

You may want manila folders to fit in the hanging folders, though it is not necessary to put them in the hanging folders. You will need self-adhesive filing labels to put on your manila folders.

The problem with files is twofold—the problem of putting things into the file (we procrastinate on this job) and the problem of getting them out (that is, finding material easily after you have filed it). Never fear—I found just the thing for both problems. Both are well worth the small price they cost.

1. Help for getting paper filed easily. Let us assume you have a file cabinet and have it all set up and ready to go. Let us also assume that many of your papers are filed, but now you have to maintain your new system. So now you begin to get papers to be filed and don't feel that you have the time to file them. At least do a little bit of prefiling by sticking them in what I call a *"lap file,"* which can be found in an office supply store (where they call it a "classification file"). That way, when you get ready to put them in the big file, most of the work is done—*and* you avoid that scary pile that will develop if you don't

145

put it in the lap file. By the way, for many people, the lap file is all that is necessary for their whole family file for a year. You might try using only the lap file before you buy a file cabinet and other accessories.

Notice that the lap file is not the accordion file with closed sides commonly found in drugstores and variety stores. Many people find the accordion file too frustrating to use because it is hard to get things out of its dark recesses. The open-sided lap file works much better.

2. Help for getting papers out easily. One reason Messies hate to file things is because they are afraid that if they put stuff in that big dark file they won't ever be able to find it again. Frankly, in my file, I keep forgetting what my headings are. As you know, Messies have such poor memories that they keep forgetting what their organizational plan is.

To solve this problem, I have what I will call a filing memory book. I use a flip-up photo album. On each of the cards I put an alphabet letter, and on that card I put all of the file folders that start with that letter. Then when I go to the file and can't remember where I might have filed a paper, I check my filing memory book so I can guess where to check first.

Paper Center: Caring for Papers

You will need letter trays to hold the papers that come into your house. The papers, mainly in the form of mail, have to have a place to go. They can't just sit on the dining room table, can they? (Well, of course, I suppose they can and probably have in the past.)

Now, however, try this method. In a convenient and easily accessible spot, keep several letter trays. (I keep mine on the telephone table in the dining room.) Label them as follows. Bills to Pay, Things to Do, Things to Read, Undecided. Put in any other trays you find necessary.

Many Other Dances

There are many other areas of the house that require some money to make things easier or more beautiful for us. There are simple things such as kitchen organization aids to hold the aluminum foil and wax paper. There are other kitchen helps like lazy Susans on shelves, plate dividers, and drawer organizers.

Along with organization aids, there are decorative changes to make like getting a new toilet seat, new knobs for the bathroom mirror, and replacing things that suddenly look shopworn now that you're taking the time and interest to actually notice them.

Looking back it is amazing how many changes are needed to remedy years of doing things the hard way.

Name or describe the location of an office supply store in your area.

What is a date you may be able to get there?

Is your phone center satisfactory? If not, list the problems and possible solutions.

Problems	Possible Solutions
_____	_____
_____	_____
_____	_____

How do you handle the papers you need to keep?

What improvement do you need to make?

What do you plan to do with bills, other mail, and papers that need handling but shouldn't be abandoned on the dining room table?

From the last chapter, make a list of things you are going to look at when you are in the office supply store. Plan to spend time browsing, but remember, buy only what you know you'll need, or you'll just have more junk in the house. Office supply stores are seductive that way.

I knew I was making progress when I walked downstairs from the bedroom and thought, "Gee, the stairs are so clean Thomas must have carried everything up," and then remembered I had done it by carrying something up each trip I made, and for once I dashed in to wash my hair in the kitchen sink and didn't have to clean out all the dirty dishes first from the night before!

Thanks for your help!

Jan / Illinois
(A sentimental, paper-loving collector)

14

Room by Room

Two special rooms are of utmost importance—the living room and your bedroom. The living room is important because it is the most public area of your house and reflects you to the world, and the bedroom because it is your special private place and reflects you for yourself.

The bathroom and the kitchen are, in their own way, public rooms and so require special handling.

The Living Room

Often, in the home of a Messie, the living room is cluttered because it is here she presents her many-faceted self and her many interests to the world. An observer can discover, just by looking around, many things about her.

She is a good mother. Many of her children's "items" are around the room—a ghastly handmade ashtray, pictures of and by the children, and maybe toys.

She is an intellectually alert person. Piles of books, magazines, and newspapers attest to that.

She is creative. Her hobby and craft equipment and resulting achievements are amply displayed.

She is cultured. DVDs, stereo equipment, and CDs in disarray indicate recent cultural interests. Who knows how recently these things were gotten out? Perhaps they have been strewn around for a long time. The piano, if there is one, has sheet music stacked on top.

She is practical. The Messie house is jammed to the rafters with so much stuff that some of it has to be stored—ever so cleverly, of course—in the living room. Maybe it's under the couch, in ugly but practical pieces of furniture, or in some other secret cache devised by the fertile Messie mind.

Messies can be happy to some extent in all that clutter because they don't really notice the overall effect it gives.

Messies suffer from tunnel vision, and even that is not too sharp. The typical Messie has no idea how the house looks to a first-time visitor. She seldom if ever looks at the room as a whole. She thinks of the meaningfulness of one piece when she buys it and adds it to the living room, seldom noting the total picture being created.

This lack of perception is found even in those Messies who are artists, sculptors, flower arrangers, decoupagers, or anyone else involved in creating beauty. The artist who has her own lovely paintings hung around her living room may not be aware that the dingy atmosphere of the room is detracting from her display.

150

In order to get the living room in order, the Messie has to "see" what is in the room. To do this, walk outside without cleaning up and imagine you are a prospective buyer or an unexpected visitor from the church you have just begun to attend. Look through your living room window. What impression do you get? Walk through the front door and look around as though for the first time.

Quickly write down your impressions, and don't lose them, because you won't be able to capture the same impressions if you try to come in for the "first time" again.

Look at the windowsills, tops of furniture, and mantelpiece. Great or gloomy?

Look at the furniture—is it too much or too old or too big or just not right for the living room? Messies usually have too much furniture. Do you?

Look at how the furniture is arranged. Can it be rearranged to better suit your purposes?

Look at the walls. Cluttered walls make the whole room look even more cluttered.

Finally, ask yourself if you are encouraging or permitting too many activities in the living room. Is it the children's play area, the afternoon rest and TV area, the eating area, the project area? If you have been letting so much go on in the living room that you have developed living-room overload, try to reassign some activities to other rooms—resting in the bedroom, playing in the den or kids' own rooms, eating in the kitchen or den. Perhaps moving the TV out of the living room will draw many of these activities to another room. Keep close tabs on the activities that remain—immediately remove cups and plates after eating, have the kids take their toys back quickly, put away books being read, and never, never dump stuff in the living room as you come in the front door.

If it is more convenient for you to have certain activities in the living room such as eating, make sure you control these by having coasters for drinks and, to the best of your ability, easy-to-clean furniture and carpets.

Don't be afraid of empty shelves or unused space.

If you want the children to play in the living room, give them a boundary in which to stay, a place to store their toys easily (perhaps in a box that rolls on coasters into the hall closet) and move fragile things out of their way.

The living room may be the room most likely to suffer from the "Terrible Too's." Too much furniture, too many mementos, too many decorations, too many activities, and too little control.

The Bedroom

Some Messies prefer to start getting control of the house in their own bedroom because it is the most personal place to them. As they seek strength to order their lives, it seems natural to begin the uncluttering and beautifying process in the bedroom. The piles of paper around the edges of the bed and on the bedside tables are ushered out. The books on the chest of drawers are given away or reshelved elsewhere. Perhaps some of the awkward furniture that has been wedged in to hold more stuff is removed. Once they start to see order, they begin to look for beauty. The bedspread and curtains are the first to be changed. On and on it goes—ugly creeps out and lovely eases in until the Messie builds that spot where she always knows she can find strength and dignity to carry her through the hard times of renovating the rest of the house. We will consider several strategic areas in the bedroom, starting with closets.

152

The closet needs to be tackled, and many items residing in there need to leave the shadow of your protection. The bedroom is frequently the place many miscellaneous items have been squirreled. Sentimental treasures are here for safekeeping and comfort. In the closet are many old, outgrown, but "good" clothes that have not been worn in more than a month of Sundays. All of these items need to go into one of four places—a box with "Give Away" written on it, a box with "Store Elsewhere" written on it, back into the closet, or, if you cannot decide about some pieces of clothing or if they belong to someone else, into a box labeled "Thinking About" with a date in the near future marked on it.

If your clothes are in the box, your mind will begin to adjust to their going away, and your spirit will begin to exult in the glorious freedom of actually having room in your closet.

When the due-date comes, you will in all likelihood happily take the box to whatever charity is closest to your house. (Remember, the easier you make it, the more likely it is that you will do it.) If you absolutely must retrieve something out of the box before it goes, you may do so. My guess is that you won't even look inside.

If the box is full of someone else's things, tell that person where the clothes are and the date they are leaving so he or she can adjust. Some wives just move their husbands' unused clothes to the basement or another closet without telling them. If they don't ever ask for them, the clothes move out to find a useful purpose in some other place. It is only fair to the clothes to help them find significance by being used. An unworn jacket is an unhappy jacket.

You will encounter shoes, purses, and hats. You will find old insurance policies, American flags, childhood mementos, and parts of collections. Put as little back into the closet as possible. Don't be afraid of empty

153

shelves or unused space. It's okay to have room for your eyes to roam without seeing something stuffed into every inch. You will get used to the strangeness of it and soon grow to love the freedom of the uncluttered way of life.

At first, organize your closet the simplest way possible. Hang all of the same kinds of clothes (blouses, skirts, etc.) together in order from the lightest-colored to the darkest-colored. Get as much up off the floor of the closet as possible by putting the shoes on an easily accessible shoe organizer. Put up hooks for hanging things you use frequently only if the hooks are easy to get to. Decide how you are going to corral all of the belts and ties. There are many convenient and easy-to-use closet accessories for this purpose. You can find them in department stores, variety stores, and so on. Initially, you may want to make a trip to the nearest store that carries closet organization accessories and buy a few standard items. Later, if you see the need and have the money, treat yourself to a professional ready-made closet kit or have your closet organized by a custom builder. Remember, however, that the less costly and time consuming your initial plan is the more likely you'll be to carry it through. Don't plan things that are too complicated. Maintain a balance. You have the rest of the house to contend with too, you know.

You will soon grow to love the freedom of the uncluttered way of life.

In the master bedroom tackle the dresser by using the same get-rid-of-and-store-what-you-can-elsewhere procedure in order to free up both the drawers and the top of the dresser.

Give thought to the beauty of the top of the dresser. Deodorants and hair spray belong in a closet or drawer along with the nail polish. Only a few decorative pieces, one of which may be the jewelry box, should be seen on top of the dresser.

Pictures are frequently a part of the dresser area. Make sure the pictures match your color décor and are ones you want, not ones you just somehow got stuck with. Make sure they are properly placed. Many people place their pictures higher up on the wall than is attractive. If yours are too high, lower them. Study decorating magazines carefully for ideas on picture placement. It makes all the difference in the world.

Inside the dresser drawers, use commercial dividers if the drawers are shallow enough for the low dividers found in most stores. If your drawers are deep, use shoe boxes to section off bras, panties, slips, stockings, and other paraphernalia. Nothing is more demeaning than having to hunt every day for enough clean undies to get dressed. Make it easy on yourself. Why let that aggravation continue? It is just this kind of chronic frustration that starts draining your energy for the day. Take control of your dresser for your own self-respect.

The same goes for jewelry. Your jewelry should be stored so it's very easy to put away and very easy to find and get out for wearing each day. This means we don't put things like hairbrushes on top of the jewelry box lid, and we don't put hairspray or books in front of the jewelry box drawers. Things like that make using the jewelry box difficult. If the organization setup is easy to use, you will use it. If your setup is awkward and requires work, it will grind to a halt and you will abandon it. Jewelry will end up piled in front of the jewelry box.

Whether or not you want to store things under your bed is up to you. If you do, buy under-the-bed storage boxes. Some are made of heavy, clear plastic for easy viewing. Some are designed to slide easily. Write in large letters on the visible side of each box what is inside so you won't have to make a fresh search each time you need something. If you use the under-the-bed boxes for storage of seasonal clothes, you can write "Cold Weather Items" on the right side of the box for summer storage and "Warm Weather Items" on the left side.

The same box can be permanently used for warm and cold clothes alternately, and the box can be turned so that the appropriate list shows from under the bed.

Let's look back over the bedroom. Has the extra furniture been removed? Are furniture surfaces and the floor clear of clutter? Are pictures well placed, and do they coordinate with the spread and curtains? Finally—is your room easy to use and to keep free of clutter? Are the closets a joy to behold and the drawers neat? In short, are you encouraged when you walk into the room? Does it bring life to your spirits?

The Bathroom

The bathroom is a small room that gets a lot of use. It needs special control. That basically means getting rid of the clutter. Bathrooms differ markedly. They range from those with ample drawers and ample cabinet space to those with no storage room at all except a small medicine cabinet over the sink. If a person is a Messie, it hardly matters how much space there is because all surfaces and spaces will be overused and cluttered. The trick is to pare down all the junk—makeup, hair curlers, blow dryers, brushes, and so forth.

Many of these items should be stored in other places. My medicine is in the kitchen; my curling iron and blow dryer are on hooks in the hall closet. My makeup is in plastic shoe boxes in the hall closet. Some of these things should be moved to bedroom closet shelves or dresser drawers.

A woman at my self-help group was sharing her foray into the bathroom. "I spent two weeks camping in the Rockies recently," she said. "I had only one little cosmetic bag of makeup and every day I looked beautiful. When I got home, I asked myself why I needed this room full of lipsticks, creams, and lotions. So I got rid of them, and now my bathroom is wonderful to be in!"

Somewhat sheepishly she added, "I didn't throw them out exactly. I packed them in a box and put them away." Well, at least it was a good beginning. Her mind is adjusting to their going, but it's hard to get rid of cosmetics because you have to throw them away. (Nobody wants to adopt used cosmetics!)

Try to remove everything possible from the bathroom, including the dirty clothes hamper and bathroom scale. Our family bathroom has only one small medicine cabinet for toothpaste and shaving stuff, and it is enough.

Now, in the place of clutter, look for ways to add beauty. An appropriately colored picture, an additional mirror perhaps. The tops of the toilet tank, bathroom windowsill, and tub corners should be empty. Shampoos and conditioners should go on a shower caddy, and children's bath toys should be stored in a mesh bag and hung on the caddy.

If you have a tub/shower combination with a shower curtain, consider this treatment. It involves hanging window curtains on a tension rod. It is possible to use regular window curtains, but the idea has been adapted and packed in shower curtain form as well. Look for them in the bath section of department stores or in bath shops. The shower curtain liner slides behind the curtain on the shower curtain rod, leaving the decorative tension rod curtain in place.

The nicest part of any bathroom is the clear and shining fixtures. When all of the clutter is gone, these are easy to keep sparkling and, as a result, sanitary.

The Kitchen

Like the bathroom, the kitchen has a tendency to attract ugly and useless clutter. Drawers are filled with a profusion of melon ballers and cola caps along with plastic ties for tying storage bags. Cabinets sport an array of seldom-if-ever-used juicers, strainers, crock pots, hot dog cookers, and what-not. Cooking paraphernalia is hard to part with because cooking is such a nurturing thing to do. We are emotionally attached to cooking. However, we must clear the insides of the cupboards, because otherwise we will meet frustration getting things out and so much resistance putting things away that we will end up just leaving them out on the counter.

The kitchen is divided into several centers, the dish center and the cooking center being the basic ones. At the dish center should be the sink and dishwasher, the shelves for dishes, and the drawers for silverware. In the cooking center should be the stove and microwave, pots and pans, and food and spices. This is the ideal. Obviously, you will not tear up your kitchen tomorrow to reach it. The thing you can do is to make sure that your kitchen is the best it can be as it is now constructed.

Very few kitchen setups are perfect, but most can be improved with thought. Make two signs, one that says "Dish Center" and another "Cooking Center." Tape them in the middle of each center. Then step back and evaluate. If you find that your centers are spread everywhere, check to see what you can do to consolidate them. *Then do it.*

Now comes the important part—counter clear-off and beauty. The counter must be absolutely as clear as possible—the best is totally clear.

Here are things that should not be stored on the counter:

electric mixer
microwave
toaster
electric can opener
canister set
knife holder block
and the ever-present etc.

"But," you ask, "how can I do this?" Very simply—for the microwave, mixer, and toaster, get the kind that go under the cabinets. As a matter of fact, there are now lots of appliances designed to be attached under the cabinets. There are even drawers and attachments. As soon as possible, move the old appliances out and the under-the-cabinet appliances in. In the meantime, store what you can underneath in the cabinets, even if it seems awkward to do so.

Let me say a word about the electric can opener. It is such an unpleasant, noisy machine that I threw mine out in favor of a good quality hand-operated can opener that fits easily in a drawer.

The kitchen walls are important too. They should not be cluttered with hanging pots or calendars. Put the pots in a cabinet if there is any room at all and put the calendar and its accompanying notes and pencil inside a cabinet door. I know restaurant kitchens hang pots from the walls and ceiling, but they are not aiming for a lovely décor.

At this point, you will be thinking that I am being too extreme in encouraging counters be made clear and walls free of pots. I know that in magazines you see beautiful pictures of stylish kitchens with bowls of fruit, baskets of flowers, baskets of fake eggs, jars full of colored macaroni, and jars crammed with cooking utensils on the kitchen counter.

In the first place, these are pictures especially set up for the magazine photographer. There are, however, some people who live in kitchens exactly like this. Every time you go into their kitchen, you will think the Better Homes and Gardens staff is arriving any minute. They have clever decorations sitting around in their kitchens—why can't we?

Decorations like this are to Messies what sugar is to a diabetic. Most people can eat sugar without problems; diabetics have to restrict their sugar intake because they can't handle it. Messies have to resist having too many decorations and appliances on the counters and walls because we can't handle it visually. Anything on the counter encourages us to add to it. Besides, Cleanies have the patience to lift the items and clean under them. Messies do not. Trust me, a clear counter encourages order.

What can we do to have a beautiful kitchen?

What can we do to have a beautiful kitchen? After streamlining the cabinets inside and the counters and walls as much as possible, consider how you may decorate tastefully.

Window treatment. Here is a place to pick up the colors you are using by choosing attractive curtains, shades, or miniblinds.

Wall treatment. Choose an appropriate and color-coordinated hanging or picture.

Counters or windowsills. Choose one thing—silk flowers in a basket, perhaps—for the visual focal point.

Move carefully to bring controlled order and beauty to your kitchen. It will bring big rewards.

We could go on and on about the kids' rooms, about the den or family room, about the basement and garage, and all types of closets.

However, if you can get these four basic rooms under control by using the order and beauty principles mentioned here and if you can use your successes in these rooms as a springboard of enthusiasm, these other areas will follow behind, slowly but surely.

Remember, each room is a unique canvas on which you can paint your personality. What a challenge! What an opportunity!

part 5

Interior Design
for the Messie

15

What? A Messie Decorator?

We Messies need to approach decorating our homes with the same patient attention that we gave de-messing our homes. And we really need someone who understands our dilemma to show us how. That is why I am so pleased to introduce to you Rebecca Emerick. Rebecca is a member of the American Society of Interior Designers (ASID) and has operated her own interior design studio, The Village Atelier, for many years. She really knows interior design.

But that's not the best part. Rebecca is a former Messie! She got in touch with me after she read *The Messies Manual* to tell me how helpful it had been to her. As we talked, it became very clear that she could be a real help to us Messies. Her ideas and suggestions on how to discover your own special personality in decorating your home are fresh and exciting—and very manageable. She teaches her MAGIC ROOM concept in lectures and adult education seminars, so I've asked her to give us the basics, just to get us started.

A suggestion before you start: Remember, things take time, and good things take more time. Have patience with yourself and your home and don't try to do everything all at once. If you expect to be able to do everything overnight or even in a week, you are going to find yourself very frustrated and maybe even quit right in the middle of things. Build the time into your plans to achieve your goals—the time needed to plan, to shop, to paint, sew, refinish, and the time needed to find the dollars in your budget. Your house did not get Mount Vernonized overnight—your home won't be decorated overnight. Do a little at a time, enjoy what you do, and keep at it.

Rebecca Emerick

Yes. One year ago I ordered *The Messies Manual* and actually put my house in order. It wasn't easy, but the results were heartening—people who see my house now would never guess the awful truth. I was a professional interior designer who ran an interior design business for years with my best friend, also an interior designer and a Cleanie. We were a good team—I wrote the advertising, and she sorted the bills and kept the door to my office shut. I also was an expert who gave talks and lectures and taught classes at the local recreation center on interior design. How could I hide my true propensities for so long? Easy—I was a "Closet Messie," the kind whose living room looks fabulous but whose hall closet is a lethal booby trap for any unfortunate who tries to hang up his coat.

As a professional interior designer and a Messie, I am in a unique position to understand the special problems we have in getting our houses in order. Sandra Felton, when asking me if I could write these chapters, said, "I don't believe that a person could be motivated to clean her house if it's not pretty when she finishes," and I certainly agree. Messies sometimes feel so bad because they are messy that they fail to imagine the beautiful rooms that they really deserve. This condition is called the "failure of the imagination," and fighting this condition is our first priority.

What Is Failure of the Imagination?

Failure of the imagination is a terrible kind of malaise that grips us when the living room is covered with dust and old magazines and children's train sets and cat hair. It is a disease that strikes the unwary Messie who thinks that if she could just get it all cleaned up once, everything would be all right. But then what would she have when she's done? Perhaps a tidy, bare living room. Inoffensive—yet uninspiring. We need to be uplifted and buoyed by the beauty of our surroundings, not bored and depressed. But before we can even get the energy to clean out a space, we have to have a beautiful mental picture to inspire us toward getting out the wheelbarrow and going at it. This vision is of the MAGIC ROOM.

What Is the MAGIC ROOM?

The MAGIC ROOM is the room we all deserve. Look at the rooms in the home fashion magazines—these

167

are MAGIC ROOMS. We can imagine living some kind of wonderful life in each of them. One room says, "I am glamour, I am fun, I am all white satin and cream for rugs and clear Lucite tables and a single orchid." Or a family room says, "I am all masculine leisure—stone fireplace, bear rug, antiqued leather sofas, and oak-paneled walls." Another room breathes, "I am the nursery, I am innocence and lace and lullabies, a soft tinkle of Brahms on an antique music box. I am love and pink fuzzy blankets and little pillowcases embroidered with 'Now I lay me down to sleep'." We've all admired rooms like these, so why not have one of your own? Anybody can. Believe me, it's just a matter of reading on and tackling the problem step by step.

> The MAGIC ROOM is the room we all deserve.

Fighting Failure of the Imagination

Finding your personal style. This is important—a leopard can't change her spots, apparently as far as interior decorating is concerned. The furniture we choose, the rug we fancy, the colors we crave—all have their roots in specific personality traits. To go against the grain of your personal taste creates a lot of psychological strain. We all have said, "I just couldn't live with that." We mean it—we really couldn't live with some things, and we shouldn't try.

A test I use for deciding if a certain piece looks good or whether I even like it, is to put the piece in an unexpected place—an antique Chinese vase on the kitchen counter, for instance, and then try to forget I put it there. In the middle of the night, coming down for a peanut butter sandwich, I switch on the light, and in that instant of surprise, I see the object truly. In a flash, I react emotionally to the piece rather than intellectually, and I flash instant love or indifference or hate. It is on this level—of the immediate subconscious reaction—that you have to like something. It is a reaction so fast, it doesn't even seem to be connected to thought—I call it the "happy eye." If something doesn't give you the happy eye, don't talk yourself into thinking you like it. I bring up the happy eye because I suspect many Messies don't want to clean up the house because they don't have anything that they feel strongly enough about to want to see clean.

This discussion has nothing to do with money—obviously we could all improve our homes with limitless funds. My intent is to analyze the factors under our control. If a person has misjudged her personal style and is unhappy with the result, if a person has gotten stuck with a lot of noxious hand-me-downs and doesn't have the nerve to resist, if a person has given up on creating a suitable personal setting because she can't control her personal clutter—this is the person I'm addressing. Having no money to do with certainly can be a complication, but it's one that virtually all of us face. I'm interested in helping with the underlying hang-ups that keep us from ever effecting any changes. Money, or the lack of it, is secondary. First you have to know what you want to do!

Anyway, many Messies have the problem of not caring about their houses. Whatever the reason, they have abdicated any personal identification with their homes and feel little emotional involvement with their decorating. I've noticed some reasons that this happens, and I'll share them with you. Then I'll show you how to analyze your personal style effectively and create a home you care about. First take this little test.

Seek simplicity. Seek nature. Seek a rhythm of living. Seek beauty. Seek quality.

Finding Your Personal Style

Test Your Messie Decorating Style

Yes	No	
Yes	No	Did your husband and five-year-old son pick out your dining room set because you couldn't make up your mind and twelve people were coming for Thanksgiving dinner? See "The Aesthetically Deprived Child."
Yes	No	Are you unable to make any decorating decisions because you are afraid the result would be dull and ordinary? Do your rooms have to be so fabulous that you have nothing in them yet? See "The Fabulous Syndrome."
Yes	No	Does dear, departed Aunt Agatha's lace antimacassar rest on an ancient black-vinyl sofa your husband bought long before you were married? Did your mother-in-law insist on adding her old Chinese modern TV cabinet and Great-Uncle Harry's worn-out plaid recliner to this, your family room? See "The Hand-Me-Down Victim."
Yes	No	Do you think that Intaglio is a skin disease that your kids pick up at school? Do you think Chippendale is a couple of cute little squirrels who sing Christmas carols? See "The Busy-Career-Woman Syndrome."
Yes	No	Do you hate all your furniture, loathe all your accessories, resent all your rugs, and secretly hope for another biblical flood so you can start over after the waters recede? Do you feel that people with beautiful houses care too much about appearances and probably terrorize their children on the sly? See "The Nonmaterialist Syndrome."
Yes	No	Do you have trouble visualizing which car you took to the supermarket after you emerge laden with groceries? Can you easily recall an image of your last dog? See "The Nonvisualizer Syndrome."

The Aesthetically Deprived Child

The Aesthetically Deprived Child's name is legion—I have had several clients in this category, and their main difficulty is a total inability to make up their minds. And why can't they make up their minds? Because behind every thought they have, before any emotion can emerge from that murky subconscious—Mother speaks! Do you *really* like that? Don't you really like this better?

Mother may have gone to her reward years ago, but she still hamstrings every decision. Her voice is always in the back of the mind, commenting on every purchase. "That isn't quite right, dear." "That color makes you look ill." "Where did you learn that?"

> To achieve great results in our houses, we have to be a little daring.

Children whose taste is ever fostered, who hear their selections corrected by Mother (or Father or Uncle Fred or whoever brings them up) often grow up afraid to make decisions. As long as they don't pick it out, they can't fail. Often they relegate decorating decisions to others in the household, hoping to avoid the stress of making a wrong decision. But this is often unsatisfactory because the husband or child or mother—if she's still around—has different tastes, and the hapless Aesthetically Deprived Adult is trapped in an environment she didn't select and doesn't like.

Since the Aesthetically Deprived Adult fears that any decision she makes which results in the concrete acquisition of a decorative object will just prove what a tasteless creature she is, she needs to keep one thing in mind: to achieve great results in our houses, we have to be a little daring.

One client of mine was so afraid to decorate that her living room had been completely empty since she'd moved into her house five years earlier. Her husband wanted to entertain, and she felt awful because she couldn't decide what she wanted.

"What would you have if you lived all alone and didn't have to please anybody but yourself?" I asked.

171

She thought a minute and said, "You know, it's silly, but I've always liked pictures of puppies." She actually blushed.

"What kind of puppies?"

"Cocker spaniels," she said. "But I don't dare put cocker spaniel pictures all over the living room. And the other thing I like are those big English wing chairs with flowered chintz all over them." She had described, of course, the basic elements of an English country-style look, a potentially charming room. Further examination revealed a suppressed taste for red and a secret yen for an oriental rug. She couldn't imagine how all of this could go together, but it did. We used a dark blue and red oriental rug and two big wing chairs blooming in a red, cream, and blue-flowered chintz. Flanking a bowl of flowers on the mantel sat twin Staffordshire figures of, what else, cocker spaniels! Everyone loved it and said, "Where did you find those adorable porcelain dogs? They just make the room."

So don't be afraid to exert your true personal taste. The best rooms come from the heart, not a consensus of what's in this year and what your neighbors like. Making a successful interior design statement depends on daring to be original. Rooms with lots of personality must get that personality from you, dear reader. So press on. The real challenge is in deciding what your personal taste really is if you never dared think about it.

The Fabulous Syndrome

A variation of the Aesthetically Deprived Child is the Five-Pound Chicken Trying to Lay a Ten-Pound Egg. She has what amounts to decorator's block because she isn't content to do something well; it has to be fabulous. Like the Perfectionist Messie, she would rather do nothing than something that is not up to her perfectionist standards. So, she does nothing. Paradoxically, the Five-Pound Chicken Trying to Lay a Ten-Pound Egg does her best work when she isn't trying so hard trying to do everything so outrageously wonderful that her efforts can backfire. As in many other enterprises, a relaxed approach can lead to better results.

The Hand-Me-Down Victim

The Hand-Me-Down Victim is sometimes poor, or poorer than her rich relations. Sensitive and sentimental, she dislikes hurting other people's feelings. So she gets a lot of strange donations, usually from her husband's family, although I know of one who got a particularly loathsome estate from her own favorite uncle. She loved the uncle too much to get rid of the furniture. A guilt legacy is unusual, though. More often the lucky recipient "just happens to need a new sofa. I know you'll just love this. It's too good to throw out." Needless to say, it's not good enough to keep either, but the Hand-Me-Down Victim has both a dire need for a sofa and an inability to say no.

> "These I have loved: white plates and cups, clean— gleaming."
>
> —Rupert Brooke

The Hand-Me-Down Victim must fight back or be inundated in junk and peculiar antiques. The two best weapons are outright refusal and subterfuge.

If the donation is really shot, just refuse it. Such offers are vaguely insulting, anyway, but usually emanate from well-intentioned relatives who just hate to throw things out.

If the piece is valuable or a sentimental heirloom but not your taste, try the fading-heirloom trick. This usually works when you really don't want the piece but love the person who gave it to you and don't want to hurt feelings. A friend of mine, Celia, once received a large Victorian cabinet from a dear aunt who visited regularly. As is so often the case, the most interest in the piece is in the beginning. Celia put it in the living room and raved over both the cabinet and her aunt's generosity. Everybody admired it, and her aunt was pleased that Celia appreciated it enough to put it in a place of prominence. Three months later, Celia moved it into the hall and told Auntie that it looked perfect in there; why hadn't she thought of it in the first place! It was a long, dark hallway, and over the next three months Celia edged the cabinet down the hall. Next she was inspired to move it into the guest room: "Such a useful piece; why didn't I think of that before!" After it had been in the guest room a year, she gave it to a young relation who actually admired it—a Victorian buff. Celia told her aunt, "Much as I liked that piece, I just couldn't turn Mary Ellen down—she loved it so much, she cried when I gave it to her."

All were evasions, of course, except that Mary Ellen really did want the cabinet badly. This technique often works well for saving people's feelings. So just be grateful at the onset, and then keep edging that gift down that hall!

The Busy-Career-Woman Syndrome

Many women have literally never had time to look around at the home-furnishings market to see what they would like if they could redo their own houses. Harried young mothers and ambitious career women fall into this category. They work so hard and focus so narrowly on one aspect of their lives that they forget they deserve a beautifully decorated home. I remember Leslie, an intelligent and bubbly young woman with a demanding job and two small boys, who presented herself at our studio. "I want to redo my living room," she announced happily. "I've saved my salary for two years."

"What style do you like?" I asked, and she exploded with laughter. "I've been so busy making the money to do it, I haven't even thought about what I want." We had to spend several weeks going through design magazines and furniture catalogs and many afternoons going through the showrooms until she got an idea of what her taste really was. Suddenly one day the phone rang.

"I want a dramatic, modern living room in antique ivory and black, with lacquer red accents. I want a clean-lined black lacquer hanging unit on the fireplace wall, and I want to cover the fireplace mantel with ivory travertine and brass trim. I want an ivory sofa and a big French chair, maybe done in red. Accents of brass and glass. Maybe a brass and glass coffee table and Japanese screens behind the sofa. Just big, simple calligraphy scrolls." And after two months of looking, talking, thinking, and experimenting, it all came tumbling out: Leslie's MAGIC ROOM. After this breakthrough we put the room together very quickly. It was a knockout—sophisticated with black marble tiles in the entry and a stunning color scheme. The heavy contrasts of black and ivory made a fabulous background for art and flowers.

So take heart, too-busy Messies—you can develop your own taste rapidly once you direct your energy toward design appreciation.

The Nonmaterialist Syndrome

There was an interesting study done not long ago of the ratio between the number of decorative objects a person had and the number and quality of her personal connections to other people. In other words, who would have more friends: the Spartan type who had few decorative objects and toys around and even fewer that she really prized or the free spirit living with pounds of clutter? The people with the fewest objects, the fewest knickknacks, toys, artworks, and collections maintained that they prized people, not things. They were not materialistic, they said, and that's why they didn't like a lot of junk around. However, the study found that the cluttered souls, up to their necks in bric-a-brac, had many more friends, more family connections, and more active social and civic ties than the other group.

Messies are nicer than other people.

This is good news for Messies, of course, and it confirms one of our favorite secret beliefs—that Messies are nicer than other people. But it's really true in my professional experience that the potential clients who had the most clutter were the easiest to work with, provided that they liked the clutter. One of the tests my associate and I use on our initial interview at the client's home to determine if we want to take the job is to ask, "What object in this room is your favorite?" If the person is hard put to identify anything as her favorite or to show any love at all for anything she has, we always decline the job. We always suspect a person who says, "Oh, I don't really like any of it," will be a difficult client.

It's not good to have a lot of things around that you don't really like, so if you see yourself in this picture, think back to a time when you did see things you wanted. What happened? When did you decide you weren't worthy of objects and furnishings that made your heart go pitty-pat? If you have the "unhappy eye" in every direction you look in your room, it's time to really clean house!

The Nonvisualizer Syndrome

When household appearance gets below a certain level, the Messie tunes it out and loses interest. This process comes from visual tune out. The nonvisualizer just has trouble registering everything that's in front of her. A Messie whose house is a wreck can literally lose her decorating taste. By continually tuning out the unattractiveness of her environment she effectively kills her sense of visual enjoyment.

Inspiration seldom comes to those wearing psychological blinders against their everyday clutter. Before a Messie can decide what does go into her house, she needs to eliminate everything that definitely *doesn't* go. Dead houseplants, a worn-out chair you've put off covering, stained carpets, and overflowing wastebaskets—all these distractions get between us and our MAGIC ROOM.

There is a difference, of course, between visual tune out as a strategy for surviving in a mess and the inability of some people to see pictures in their mind. I've had many clients who could recite their Social Security numbers backwards or identify musical notes with perfect pitch but couldn't visualize a chair made larger or a printed fabric in another color. This is just a different kind of mind and has nothing to do with intelligence (although it is related to design ability). What is the nonvisually oriented person to do? How can she visualize her MAGIC ROOM if she can't hold pictures in her mind? Easy—collect pictures in her decorating box. These pictures will fix her own ideas in her mind and will also help her communicate her ideas to others. Often the nonvisually oriented have a ghastly time trying to explain to anyone else what something they want looks like. It's like a tone-deaf person humming a tune to a friend who keeps asking her to hum it again—and again—and again!

Those of you who have trouble visualizing can benefit by the next chapter. We talk about analyzing your personality and lifestyle so you can get a grip on your taste. Then you can find examples of what you do like, put all the pictures together, and work toward implementing your finished vision. In my third chapter we look at specific problems Messies have in implementing their visions, problems of gaining practical knowledge and planning to get around our natural proclivities.

> "With regard to excellence, it is not enough to know, but we must try to have and use it."
>
> —Aristotle

These syndromes spotlight six characteristics that may be part of our approach to decorating, our "failure of imagination." They are

- Aesthetically Deprived Child
- The Fabulous Syndrome
- Hand-Me-Down Victim
- The Busy Career Woman
- The Nonmaterialist
- The Nonvisualizer

It may be that you see something of yourself in several or all of them.

Review them, and starting with the one you feel is most characteristic of yourself, list the syndromes in order of importance. Then, in order to personalize it, include a sentence explaining briefly how you feel it applies to you. Omit any you don't feel apply to you at all.

1. _____

_____

_____

_____

_____

2. _____

_____

_____

_____

_____

3. _____

_____

_____

_____

_____

4. _____

_____

_____

_____

_____

5. _____

_____

_____

_____

_____

6. _____

_____

_____

_____

_____

16

Making Your Own
MAGIC ROOM

We have all walked into rooms and thought, This room says "comfort," or this room oozes sophistication, or this room shouts "cold person." I am asking you to do this in reverse—instead of figuring out what you want your room to say and then trying to find objects and colors and forms to say it, first figure out what you actually like, and then let your choices make the statement about your personality. This way you don't get misled by the person you think you are but let your true taste surface. (Don't be afraid. We Messies are usually much nicer than we think!)

To analyze your own taste, try this fun exercise called the Decorating Box.

The Decorating Box

Find a large cardboard box. Then just start wandering around the house and garden looking for colors you like and collect samples of them. Leafing through magazines and catalogs is your best bet. So just look at color, not subject matter. Cut out the pages with colors that interest you and label them—my favorite pink, great gray-blue, and so on. Then look around the house for pieces of fabric or wood or flowers or fruits that you like. The garden is a good place because it is full of the clear, fresh colors of nature and unexpected combinations that can inspire interesting color schemes. Don't worry now about which color goes with which; just gather up all the colors that appeal to you. Keep in mind that color schemes can be made up of all sorts of strange combinations—fortunately, people naturally like hues that go together. That means your favorite colors will probably be comfortable with one another.

When you're done you will have a box perhaps a little like Allison's. Her last child had gone off to college, and she was converting his room into an office for her business. Allison, a widow, works at home and was looking forward to having more room to spread out her paperwork. She had no idea how she wanted to do the office, which had hardwood floors and a small wrought-iron balcony beyond French doors.

"I guess I should make it look like an office," she said, without much enthusiasm. "Very practical." Since she was without any ideas on the subject of color for this room, I had her do a Decorating Box. She wandered all around the house and drew a blank. "We must have used my husband's favorite colors in the house—he liked maroon." She decided to try the backyard and came back with a daffodil and some blue hydrangeas. "I like these," she said, and put them in the box. Later, looking through magazines, Allison found a picture of a blue-and-white porcelain plate in a Blue Willow pattern and added it to the box. A search of the vegetable drawer produced a butter lettuce—"I like this color green." Allison and I gazed into the Decorating Box. "You'd better hurry up and finish the room before the box wilts," I said. We found a magazine picture of some daffodils, a botanical print to replace the real jonquils and hydrangeas, and cut a piece of lettuce-green cotton to stand in for the lettuce.

"I don't see what this adds up to," Allison said, but I urged her on to the next step.

After you have found all your favorite colors, start working on the other categories. Look through magazines and catalogs and cut out objects and treatments that catch your eye—pictures of rugs you like or flower arrangements or reproductions of paintings. Find examples of window treatments, shades, valances, lighting fixtures, and accessories.

Then look around your house for examples of different textures that appeal to you—pieces of fur or silk; the crunchy, natural feeling of a sisal doormat; the smooth, reflective surface of crystal; the icy elegance of the marble on your pastry board. Put these into your box, too, if you can get them loose. A picture of marble will do, for instance, and a small, polished wood sample can stand in for the wood you like so much on the coffee table. Look at the clothes—your husband's tweed jacket may be one of your favorite textures or the lace on your blue slip.

Now you have samples of colors, ideas, objects, and textures in your Decorating Box.

Allison's collection included her grandmother's quilt— a Wedding Ring design in delphinium, cobalt, and blueberry blue on white; a picture of a romantic Victorian love seat, very ornate with a heart-shaped back and scroll-like rolled arms; and a picture of an antique garden trellis. Allison also found a piece of soft cotton fabric she liked for texture and an entire potted fluffy ruffle fern. "I like the feeling of living, growing plants," she said. Also into the box went a picture of an old-fashioned sun porch with overstuffed sofas and potted palms.

"This is fun," Allison said, "but I should have used a refrigerator box."

"Don't worry, we're done collecting for now. Next we'll play an association game."

Using a dime-store binder with large pages, make a little scrapbook of your finds. Scotch tape a cutting or a picture of each item in your box.

After each entry, make a list of what you like about the sample. Look at the color—what does it say to you? What do the objects mean to you? Jot down quickly a list of what that color or object or texture "says"—a list of feelings and associations. Figure out and say exactly what it is that you like about it.

Allison did, and her list looked like this:

Daffodils—yellow, sunshine, spring, new beginnings

Blue hydrangea—Grandmother's veranda, quiet of a summer afternoon, tranquility

Blue Willow plate—true blue, home cooking, blue flowers, contentment

Butter lettuce—tender growing things, spring garden

Blue-and-white quilt—true blue, love from Grandmother to me, loyalty

Victorian love seat—keepsake, old wicker porch furniture

Antique garden trellis—romantic old gardens

Blue cotton fabric—soft, unpretentious, familiar, comfortable

Fluffy ruffle fern—soft, frilly, indoor garden, alive and
growing, needs TLC

Potted palm—old-fashioned conservatory, Victorian
sun porch, romantic and frilly

Allison and I studied her list. "Now, summarize what
you have said. Certain descriptions recur. You seem to
want a room that is old-fashioned, romantic, and symbolic
of spring and fresh starts, an unpretentious, comfortable
room that radiates love and a sort of loyal sentimentality—
you are a "true blue" person. The colors and textures you
have chosen reveal the person that you
really are." Allison's list reflects her loyal
disposition and giving nature as well as
her nurturing spirit and unpretentious,
friendly personality. Allison had been a
pediatric nurse before she married and
now does medical transcriptions for a
volunteer organization benefiting disabled children.

**How can I connect
what I need with
what I want?**

"So, I'm sentimental. I knew that! What does that
have to do with my office? How can I translate a list of
adjectives into sofas and chairs and desks?"

"Easy," I said. "First you make a list of furniture and
accessories you need for the room."

"I need a sofa and a big chair to relax in—this will
be a sitting room for me as well as an office. Actually,
I'd like to use that big, fat, ugly brown chair I already
have. It's perfectly good. And I need a desk, of course.
I have my typing chair; it's no beauty, but it supports
my back. I have to have a bookcase for my medical
dictionaries and a big table to spread my work out on.
That's all! How can I connect what I need with what
I want?"

"Start with the color scheme," I said. "Blueberry,
lettuce green, and jonquil yellow. What you're going
to do is apply the colors in your list to the room. You

could paint the walls a pale lettuce green, and while the paint is wet, "comb" it with a notched brush to give it an interesting, organic-looking stripe—like the subtle veins in a leaf. Throw the blue-and-white quilt over the old brown chair to make a casual kind of slipcover, and if you search the thrift shops, you should be able to find an old Victorian love seat to use for a sofa. Paint it white and add big, soft, downy pillows in the same porcelain blue as the quilt."

> Whatever is true, whatever is noble, whatever is right, whatever is pure, whatever is lovely, whatever is admirable—if anything is excellent or praiseworthy— think about such things.
>
> —Philippians 4:8 NIV

Allison started getting the idea and took off on her own: "For a desk, I could get a Victorian rolltop with flowers carved on the lid. It is informal and has a sentimental look of an heirloom, even if it is not. The medium-oak color goes well with the hardwood floor, and the lid can come down and hide my messy work in progress. I could keep my pens, pencils, and erasers in the Blue Willow porcelain jars and teapots on top of the desk." (Blue Willow is another thrift shop treasure, available for a song.)

I chimed in again, "Put a faience 'cabbage' bowl on the coffee table and fill it with jonquils, hydrangeas, and spring flowers. Your list had a lot of garden illusions, so open the French doors and plant bulbs in a white trellis planter on the balcony—that will bring the outdoors in."

Allison began searching and gathering her finds. By going out to shop with her list of adjective descriptions, she was able to find pieces that fit the mood of the room and eliminate those that didn't. She found an antique white crochet throw and made a slipcover for her typewriting chair. Instead of a green faience bowl, she found a terrific old white wrought-iron glass-topped coffee table, very Victorian, scrolly and charming, that had a planter box underneath for—what else—fluffy ruffle ferns. The room turned out magically perfect—whimsical and full of personality—specifically, Allison's personality. Going into this MAGIC ROOM, you don't get a lot of single, contradictory visual impressions of quilts and wicker and flowers. You just feel one big effect—because everything in the room contributes to the atmosphere. The room projects a definite, clear-cut mood, and thereby it makes a coherent statement. This is the definition of the MAGIC ROOM—the room itself must give a coherent visual impression rather than be seen as a collection of unrelated objects.

All of the objects in Allison's room related to her theme—the sentimental, keepsake look, with flowering plants and spring colors. If she had tried to introduce a Norfolk pine tree in a black lacquer planter, it would have muddled the message of her room. What does a Norfolk pine say? Strength, nobility, snow, cold weather, masculine vitality. All interesting characteristics, but they weren't on Allison's list. So, she put a palm tree in the corner in a blue-and-white porcelain fishbowl. People can come into Allison's office and get an immediate and strong impression of what she is about. Whether or not they like it isn't important—their tastes may be different—the important thing is that they say, "Oh, what an interesting room. It seems like spring in here, and this is February!" or "This reminds me of my grandmother's sun porch. I loved that room."

A year later, a doctor came by to drop off some typing for Allison, sat down in the quilt-covered chair, and didn't want to get out. They were married in March and covered the church in jonquils. Allison still maintains it was the room that charmed him first, and, you know what, it may be true! The really surprising thing is that when every element in the room contributes positively to the image you have in mind, you always wind up with an effect even more successful than you dared to hope.

If a room expresses your character traits truly, it winds up being an advertisement for yourself—Allison's Victorian garden room explained her nature much better than the practical office look she originally had in mind. Moreover, a successfully done MAGIC ROOM can influence more than opinions. It can change moods and contribute to your physical well-being.

This is the MAGIC ROOM in action. Not only does it exemplify all the feelings you want to express, it actually creates these feelings in others as well. I have always believed that a depressing, miserable, hostile room can make people feel and act worse, but I've never been sure to what extent positive surroundings can improve a person's life. I suspect that a room that supports a person's positive attributes, a room that says, "Yes, I am friendly, capable, and intelligent," for instance, at the very least, can give a person a positive backup, a little emotional reinforcement, and momentum.

People do identify you with your surroundings, and being identified with beautiful, pleasant surroundings is certainly better than being associated with an incoherent mess. So figure out what you are or want to be, and say it with your home—you may actually improve your own mood and performance in the process.

This chapter calls for action steps. Obtain:

- a Decorating Box to begin gathering relevant items and
- a dime-store binder to make a decorating scrapbook.

You can begin this information gathering before you are organized enough to start decorating because it may take some time for you to fully develop your personal tastes. Just start. Modify as you go along and learn your own personal tastes.

At this point, you may want to note your thoughts about your own personal tastes. Just be aware that you may find these initial ideas changing as you fill your box and notebook.

_____

_____

_____

_____

_____

_____

17

Decorating for a Cleaner Lifestyle

You should have completed a Decorating Box of your own and have a good understanding of the mood and atmosphere you want your MAGIC ROOM to reflect. You have a list of furniture and decorative accessories you would like to use and some idea of background treatments—wall color, rug styles, drapery treatments. This is the most basic task in enhancing the beauty of your home—deciding what you want. The vision of the MAGIC ROOM inspires us to action, and that is half the battle won.

But a Messie faces special problems in decorating. She must, on the one hand, conceive of a MAGIC ROOM, the vision of which inspires her to action, and yet her vision is almost always purely aesthetic. Unlike the Cleanie, she never dreams about a grand broom closet or a practical desk for paying bills. Messies seldom give any thought to the cleaning or maintenance requirements of the furnishings they choose, plan for enough storage space, or arrange their houses for convenience. Some seem fatally attracted to the most impractical things. So the question becomes "Can a Messie have a MAGIC ROOM that is practical and easily maintained?"

Practical Maintenance

The Messie is not impractical. She is often just a-practical. One example was Arabella. Arabella did her Decorating Box and brought it to our studio. "This is going to be a fabulous room," she said and started pulling out samples. Arabella's collection included:

- A piece of luscious white satin—"for my sofa and my draperies."
- A picture of an orchid garden—"I want lots of orchids around."
- A carpet sample in deep, plush, white wool.
- A catalog picture of a white lacquer coffee table.

You should know that Arabella has three children and a dog, and they all use the living room.

I took a deep breath. "These are beautiful, Arabella! This room will be stunning. We may run into a few maintenance problems, though. Have you thought about how you're going to clean a white satin sofa? One spilled cup of coffee, and it's all over. The rug will be difficult to clean as well. A cold drink left on a lacquer table will leave a ring. You can't just touch up rings on lacquer like you can on wood furniture—the whole table must

---

Felton's Law

"Any Mess That Can Happen, Will.*"*

---

be refinished, and it's very expensive. And orchids won't bloom in that room; there's not enough natural light."

As I talked, I could see Arabella's face fall. You can imagine how she felt. All her ideas (and hopes) were flying out the window.

"You told me I could have anything I wanted. How can I have my MAGIC ROOM with practical things I don't like? I don't want to be practical if it means giving up all my ideas. I want a contemporary, glamorous, sophisticated, all-white room with lots of shiny surfaces and flowing white draperies and orchids all over the place. That's what I wrote under "Theme of Room" in my Decorating Box binder. I chose white satin for the sofa because it's white and shiny and glamorous. What's the point of doing all this work if I have to get a brown Herculon sofa because of the kids?"

She was right, of course. She wanted some joy and happiness from this room, not simply endurance and reliability.

So I challenged her. "Now that we know your goals and the potential hazards, let's try to find a solution."

Her smile returned.

In the notebook Arabella had put together, she had pasted each item she liked on a separate page. The picture of the white satin sofa occupied one page with a note to the side which read "soft, white, shiny, glamorous, and sophisticated."

Let's go back to our notebooks for a moment. Remember that I said to leave some extra space on each page? You'll need room to make two more lists—a list of all the cleaning characteristics and one of all the maintenance needs for each piece that you selected for your MAGIC ROOM. In the first column, "Cleaning Characteristics," list the cleaning requirements: What common stains can be removed from each fabric type? Do wood surfaces require special polishes? Does marble discolor easily? In the second column, "Maintenance Needs," describe the sort of work each piece needs on a daily or weekly basis. For example, what sort of maintenance is needed on Arabella's white wool rug? Lots! Daily vacuuming, weekly spot removal, and a good shampooing every other month. So the question you will need to ask yourself for each of your selections is "Am I willing to take care of this?"

Arabella, a Messie, admitted, "No, I'm not. I'd still like an all-white room. But I certainly don't intend to vacuum every day. I can't afford to throw out the sofa if the baby spills hot chocolate on it. And now that you mention it, Bobby just brought home a stray kitten, and it's been running up and down the curtains. What can we do?"

"Well, let's work on each item. For instance, the list of specifications on the white satin sofa reads "soft, white, shiny, glamorous, and sophisticated." It's the style of the sofa that is glamorous and sophisticated (a 1930s low-tufted tuxedo style) and the fabric that is soft, shiny, and white. What if you used this new glazed, glove-soft leather?—it looks like white kid but is actually quite durable. It's certainly an improvement on the white satin and makes the same visual impression. Though it looks sophisticated, it only needs wiping off with a damp cloth once a week. Spills won't hurt it. And the white lacquer table—one of the new decorator Formicas that looks like lacquer can be used for that. "Lacquer" Formica looks exactly like lacquer, but it doesn't stain or scratch, and you can clean it off with window cleaner.

The white wool rug is really unbearable to maintain. Since you have hardwood floors in the living room, why don't you bleach the floors out, stain them in one of the new off-white floor stains that still shows the wood grain, and then put on a layer of urethane? Then all you have to do is mop. The floor will look shiny and white, which was in your list, and the look is very stylish and contemporary. You can still have a rug for softness and warmth. Get a Greek flokati rug for under the cocktail table. They have a soft, deep, glamorous fur look that is perfect for your room, and they can be washed in the washing machine!"

"What about the draperies and the cat?" Arabella asked.

"You can still use white satin on the window coverings—just have shades that pull up instead of long curtains that the cat can reach. A cloud shade would be terrific—it's like a balloon shade but has a looser, more contemporary look and is very soft and glamorous—just as your list says."

"So I guess I can have everything I want after all," Arabella said, "without all that cleaning and fussing. What about the orchids? I can see that maybe it could take a little effort to keep them blooming."

"Actually," I said, "orchid plants do well in a dark room. The foliage will grow, they just won't bloom. After the orchids quit blooming, buy a good silk orchid blossom and stick it in the real orchid plant. If you tie it up to a bamboo stake and fake it up realistically, everyone will think you are a horticultural genius."

By going one step further on your Decorating Box and analyzing your furnishing choices for cleanability and maintenance, you can make modifications that make life easier yet still are consistent with your MAGIC ROOM.

Don't feel you have to make painful compromises if you're drawn to the impractical. A good interior designer can really be a help to you at this point if you need suggestions or substitutions and modifications in your scheme. There are many new fibers, materials, and stain-guard processes that can make life easier these days. If you don't have access to an interior designer, go to a large furniture store and ask about the practicality of your selections. People who work in the home-furnishings field know all the horror stories about poor wear because they are the first to hear from irate customers. Such experts can be a good help to you if you consult with them before you buy. There are also many helpful books to help you understand furnishings and decorating.

> Don't feel you have to make painful compromises if you're drawn to the impractical.

Designing the MAGIC ROOM for Function

After cleanability and maintenance concerns comes the next pitfall for Messies—inadequate storage space. To live in comfort as well as style, you must create a space plan for your MAGIC ROOM that works on the functional level as well as the aesthetic. There is no great mystery to this. Here are the steps.

- Make a list of all the functions the room must perform.
- Make a list of the furniture each function demands. (Reading needs a good light and a place to sit, for example.)
- Make a list of the storage needs for each function. (Reading needs bookcases and magazine racks as well as a chair and light.)

Felton's Laws Expanded

You will always find something in the last place you
   look.
You will remember that you forgot to take out the
   trash when the garbage truck is two doors away.
Don't call the police because your house has been
   vandalized until you are really sure.
The difference between "I can" and "I can't" is often "I
   will."
An ounce of "now" is worth a pound of "later."
There's never time to put it away, but there's always
   time to look for it.

- Now make a room sketch and draw in all the storage as well as the furniture arrangements. .

   Now your room is space-planned for practicality and
a cleaner lifestyle.
   Messies often use the defense that storage and utilitarian equipment are ugly and will ruin their "look."
But with a little ingenuity, you can achieve comfort and
convenience, neither of which needs to be at odds with
imaginative decorating. Even MAGIC ROOMs have
wastebaskets and pens and telephone books. They just
have interesting wastebaskets and pens and telephone-
book covers that harmonize with the rest of the room.
   The way we decorate our homes is a clear-cut indication
of personality. You can walk into people's houses and "read"
their personalities by the colors they've used, the furniture
they've chosen, even the way their furniture is arranged in
the room. Keep the vision of that MAGIC ROOM anchored
firmly in front of you, and you may be surprised at how
your results far surpass your wildest expectations!

195

Step into Your Own MAGIC ROOM

1. Think about the room that you are decorating. Think about how it will be used, who will use it, how you'd like it to look.

2. Begin to look around your house, through the garden, magazines, catalogs, and shops. Start collecting things for your Decorating Box.

> Collect samples of the colors you favor for your room.
>
> Collect photos of objects and room treatments that you'd like to use in your room.
>
> Collect samples of textures (fabrics, finishes, etc.) that you'd like to see in your room.

3. Using your finds, create your own Decorating Notebook for the room that you are decorating.

Write out the theme of the room. This will help you remember the function of the room and your decorating goals.

Using your collected samples, tape each one to a page of your notebook. After each one, describe why you like it: How does it make you feel? What does it say to you?

Then describe how a particular object or color would fit into your MAGIC ROOM.

Make a list of its cleaning characteristics.

Make a list of its maintenance needs.

Make a note about the financial considerations: budgets and costs.

Make notes about the time considerations: How much time will it take to get (or finish or find or afford)?

4. Using the pages that you have gathered, begin to discover your MAGIC ROOM. Start envisioning a finished

room. Discard (or put aside for another room) things that don't mesh for your room. And begin assembling your own personal **MAGIC ROOM!**

The next few pages are available for your sketches.

You may find it helpful to get the aid of a friend to help you focus on these steps, preferably someone whose house you admire. She (or maybe he) can go with you to shop. She can encourage, advise, or warn when asked by you for an opinion. A friend cuts down on nervousness and helps you keep your motivation. Obviously, you need someone who is empathetic and has people skills that work for you. There is no substitute for a good advisor.

Enter the name of a friend or two who might be helpful in your decorating quest. _____

_____

Somewhere along the way you may need more professional help. What professional decorator in your area who knows the latest in materials might be available to give you advice? List possible sources.

_____
_____
_____

part 6

Help Yourself

18

Dear Family

A Letter to the Family of a Messie

The Messie who is changing may be treated in one of several ways. Either she is given a great deal of approval and interest, she is treated with skepticism, or she is pretty much ignored while she gives it a try alone.

When your wife or mother begins this new way of life, it is possible that you, her family, may develop the unreasonable expectation that things will automatically become better. You do not realize how hard it will be to overcome years of destructive housekeeping habits. Things did not get out of control in a short time, and things will not improve overnight. It will take a long, careful building process to bring order and beauty to your home, usually for the first time. It helps to have

201

group support from other Messies who can help in the process.

Every Messie, though initially feeling alone, finds at Messies Anonymous others who have similar, and sometimes remarkably the same, problems. If your loved one joins with other Messies in groups either local or on the Internet, she may share openly her problems and feelings. Care is taken in these groups to treat all problems with discretion and sensitivity. You should take care to be considerate in talking to your Messie about household problems. Sarcastic and cutting remarks will only make things worse. While struggling to change, the Messie is particularly vulnerable.

Messies are people of extremes, and once hot on the trail of change, a Messie may begin to overdo. She may spend more time and energy (or money) than is wise. She may begin to nag you to put things back where they belong, whereas before she was much more reasonable and easy to live with. You may wish she had never started this change and may want to tell her so. You may even prefer the happy-go-lucky Messie to the hard-nosed person who has taken her place. What the family needs to realize is that this is a phase, and, although it would be better if she could approach the problem more moderately, it is brought on by her deep desire to pull out of the slump that years of chronic neglect have plunged the house into. You may feel you have patiently put up with her messes all these years, have even been trained to live in them, and now she shows no patience with you. It may seem to the children that Mom has turned overnight from a Messie into a Cleanie. She, who was once noncommittal about the house, now seems to be an evangelist of orderliness. Nothing could be further from the truth. She remains a Messie in the process of change and may be scared to death she will never make it to normalcy. That's why little messes or any lack of cooperation on your part upset her so much. She fears that her energy and resolve and vision will not last her through the long haul ahead if she meets any obstacles.

This period of adjustment is an important one and subject to much turmoil if both you and your reforming Messie are not careful. As a family, you should realize that your mother has taken a difficult step. If you can help her get through the initial battles, your life will be improved. I know she may be unreasonable and cranky with no apparent excuse for it, but caring about what she is going through will go a long way in helping her arrive at a point where the house is under control.

The reforming Messie may not remember that her husband and children have been forced to adopt a disorganized lifestyle in order to live with her all these years. Just because she has now decided that she has had enough doesn't mean they feel the same way about changing. Some, or perhaps all, of the members of your family may be naturally prone to messiness just as she is. It is true that you must not only approve of her changing, you must change as well if the house is to gain the order and beauty your reforming Messie now longs for. She has caught the vision of what your home can be; you may or may not have the same vision. She needs to show love and understanding while your whole family changes under her leadership.

Mom may feel betrayed by the family if they do not cooperate with her in her efforts. For years she has been criticized by her immediate family, in-laws, and most of all by herself. She is bewildered and frustrated when she now also receives criticism for being neater. She begins to think the real problem is that she has a critical family who just like to dump on her no matter what she does.

The Messie Manifesto
A Messie Is a Person of Dignity

A person of dignity:

- Does not keep a drawer full of hose with runs in them because sifting through them each day is demeaning. In addition, I deserve better.
- Does not wear undies with loose elastic. Nobody will know, but the person of dignity will. That's why it's important.
- Doesn't sleep on faded sheets even if they are still good.
- Doesn't allow straggly hair.
- Has clean combs and brushes.
- Doesn't wear droopy bras or dumpy housedresses.
- Keeps breath mints in her purse and uses Kleenex, not toilet paper, especially for social blowing.
- Does not make excuses for errors but accepts her own faults with dignity.
- Treats others with respect for their great value as people.
- Will not accept being "shamed" by others because of any faults, real or imagined.

The family and the reforming Messie must realize that both need to "cool it" a little during this transition period. Your family must understand that no matter how hard the change seems, you really do approve of what she is trying to do, and it will be in your best interest to encourage it. The reforming Messie needs to realize that it will take your family time to adjust to this new way of life. You may even hesitate to change because you suspect this is just a phase to ride out that won't last long.

Participation, patience, love, and caring on the part of all concerned will help to usher in a new era of family life and beauty. Mom will never be perfect, but she can attain a level of normalcy that will encourage both you and her.

Please excuse the informality of my letter, but if I don't do it now while I have paper in hand, it will get put off again. I turned in 10 minutes too late to Focus on the Family one day in June or July and heard you describing "Messies." At that time I was rushing around trying to do what I'd been trying to do all day—clean the house! I sank down by the radio and began to cry. That's me she's talking about, I thought. I didn't know there were others like me. I had thought there was something mentally or spiritually wrong with me. After the program, I rushed out to get the book—ashamed of its title. And wouldn't you know, I got an elderly, hard-of-hearing clerk and the whole store knew I was asking for a _Messies Manual._ I had been so depressed but feel maybe there's hope.

God bless you. I'm finishing your book for the 2nd time. What a help!

Dianne / Tennessee

This letter is written to the family. However, the likelihood is that you, the Messie, are the first reader.

Do you feel it is appropriate to share this letter or part of it with your family?

What ideas shared with the family about the change you are making seem to be the most applicable to you?

If you have begun making changes, are you finding unexpected resistance or problems?

In this period of transition, are there any changes you need to make in relation to your family?

Note: The book *Neat Mom, Messie Kids* (Sandra Felton) tells how to get the family to help and how to train the kids for a lifetime of organizational skills.

19

Dear Husband

A Letter to the Husband of a Messie

(Messiness is an equal opportunity problem. Men can be, and probably are, more given over to the problem of messiness than are women. The Messies Anonymous program works equally well for men who put it into practice in their lives. Men are encouraged both to start and to attend M.A. self-help groups along with women. However, since the buck for the condition of the house usually stops at the woman's tumbled desk, this chapter addresses the problem of living with a woman Messie. It is written to the husbands of Messie wives but can be applied to the wives of Messie husbands as well.)

If you are a husband of a Messie woman, whether or not she has begun to change, you have undoubtedly

207

led a difficult and unpredictable life. Over the years you may have tried various approaches to the frustration of living in clutter and chaos. Sometimes you have criticized, begged, or tried to be an example of change, only to be disappointed when things inevitably continued the same way. Occasional flare-ups of effort on her part to get the house under control have fizzled out. Against your wife's wishes, you may have hired a maid.

Messiness is an equal opportunity problem.

Coming home each evening to a house in chaos has been an effort on your part. After a hard day at work, you want peace and beauty at home, but you know you won't find it at your house. In most cases, your wife has worked hard all day either at home or at her job. You need to know that the condition of the house is even more upsetting to her than it is to you. This puts her under pressure, whether she is aware of it or not. That further strains relationships in the home. You resent the condition of the house in which you are forced to live and imagine that the homes of other men returning from work are havens of rest and order. You hesitate to invite friends over and begin to live more and more alone—scheduling social engagements at your house far in advance and even then with the fear that it will be too much trouble to get the house in order. You turn down social invitations knowing it will be difficult to repay them.

You have seen the children adjusting as best they can. You worry that they are not being trained to live orderly, beautiful lives. Will they perpetuate this as adults? you wonder. They may even now be joining in this lifestyle themselves and compounding the problem. Some may be easygoing and accept this confusion as a natural way of life. Some may be embarrassed to invite friends over and might be trying unsuccessfully to bring the house into some degree of order. It grieves you to see the problems the kids have in this kind of house.

If the truth were known, you may not be all that orderly in your way of life either. Perhaps it is your half-finished projects, your tools left out, your dropped towels, and lost keys that largely contribute to the way things are. In desperation, you may have threatened to be the biggest Messie of all and had your plan backfire when your wife was only relieved to be out from under the pressure to improve.

Naturally, you have made mistakes in trying to alter these conditions. You have been confused, frustrated, and angered. Your wife seemed powerless to change, even though she put forth effort and made many resolves. You felt that surely her pride as a wife and mother—as a woman—would help her overcome this chronic state. Would not the common sense and good judgment so evident in other things cause her to change in this area? Surely if she cared more about you and the children or understood how important it was to you, she would try harder. She shows such thoughtfulness, such caring, such warmth. When you married, she was spontaneous and fun loving—and many of these qualities remain, even in the midst of the stress of the house. Looking back on her casual attitude, you wonder now why you did not foresee some of these problems.

Perhaps the questions you had about why some people are Messies and others are not have been answered in this book. It is not from lack of caring or lack of trying that the house is in such a state. Let me encourage you that it is possible for the chronic Messie to change and provide a wonderful and gracious home.

You need to know that your part is important. You cannot make your wife change, no matter how hard you try. Neither anger nor nagging will make her want to change. Even urging her to read an M.A. book or go to

I just finished reading The Messies Manual. I can't believe how good it feels knowing that there are others like me out there. I just finished Mt. Vernonizing my downstairs bathroom and for the first time since we moved into our home I can see my kitchen counter!! My husband is thrilled. I'm starting work on my box and flipper soon. No—this is not procrastination—I'm Mt. Vernonizing the rest of the house first.

Kristine / California

a self-help group will do no good. Plant the seed. That is all you can do. The desire to change must come from within her, or it won't come at all.

You are probably aware that not all people who have disorganized houses are messy to the same degree or in the same ways. Some houses look good on the outside but are disorganized and confused in the area of storage, some houses are cluttered but manageable, some houses are under control in certain areas but have junk rooms to contend with. Some houses are out of control in every way. Some Messies suffer both from disorganized time schedules and disorganized houses, but almost all Messies have some area of order, no matter how small, in which they can take pride.

No matter what the condition of the house, it is important for you and the family to live a happy and outgoing life in as unencumbered a manner as possible. Remember and appreciate your wife's good qualities. Emphasize the important parts of your family and life. Regular church attendance will give direction to your life and help you establish your own priorities.

Do not believe that you should not move on to other aspects of life until after the house is organized. As you provide balance for yourself, you will find areas of your own life that need reordering as well. You will find that as your wife's problems begin to clear up, some of your own problems will begin to emerge. All problems will not clear up at once. There will be stops and starts.

As you begin to see improvements, both you and your wife will be elated. This is to be expected. You may now find that your hopes are dashed when she backslides or her progress is not as fast as you had wished. Previously you were willing to put up with a lot; now you lose patience at little things. Remember, your wife is overcoming habits of years and a natural tendency toward disorder.

> All problems will not clear up at once. There will be stops and starts.

New feelings bubble up within you. Long-suppressed resentment and impatience may come to the fore. She may now take over the leadership you previously provided in household management, and your ideas on household management may clash with hers.

It is hard to make any changes in life, even changes for the better. You may have grown used to not entertaining and find it difficult to change. The children may want to invite friends over, and you may not wish to be bothered. You now have the freedom to do many things involving the house that you could not do before. This freedom brings some stress to all involved, but the new life will be much better than the old one. It's worth the change.

As your wife continues her change, be enthusiastic and encouraging. Negative reactions or impatience will only discourage what you want to achieve. Once you see that she can change, you may be tempted to hurry her up in the process by lecturing or instructing. This is a mistake. Remember, only she could make the decision to begin the change, and, in the end, only she can make the decision to keep up the new way of life she has begun. And you—along with your wife and family—will reap the rewards of her decision.

I just have to tell you my story—while I was at the drug-store last weekend, I happened to come across The Messies Manual. *I had to laugh because I had just gone another round with my husband about my "not-so-wonderful" talent of housecleaning! Well, I bought it as a joke to give him, but when I got home, I started thumbing through the book and the next thing I know, I have read the whole book from front to back! I am ecstatic!*

Well, I started the "Mount Vernon Method" today—it's coming along.

Thank you for a very helpful and amusing book that helped me to acknowledge a weakness of mine, while showing the directions needed to be taken to correct it. Surprisingly enough—it actually has me looking forward to the challenge with an open mind and a much needed sense of humor!

Janet

As with the letter to the family, the letter to the husband will likely be read first by you, the Messie woman who is making a change.

Will you share this letter with your husband?

What part do you feel relates most significantly to you?
List three:

_____

_____

_____

What negative impact does your husband have on the changes you are trying to make?

What positive impact does your husband make?

20

Warming Your Coals

Starting Your Own Self-Help Group

Once there was a Messie who became warm with enthusiasm for getting her house in order. She found that all alone it was hard to maintain the desire and energy to make the change. She got an idea . . . But you know the rest of the story. That's why and how self-help groups are started.

In May 1935, Bill W., a newly reformed New York alcoholic on a business trip to Akron, Ohio, was fighting a desire to return to the alcohol that had been ruining his life. He needed someone to talk with and work with who understood his problem.

He began calling churches, hospitals, and clinics from a phone booth, searching for that person. He found Dr. Bob, a once-prominent surgeon, whose life had been

A Little Coal

Once there was a little coal who started to warm up
to the idea of getting her house in order. How happy
she was! As time went by, however, she began to yearn
for more heat to help her accomplish her goals. She
began to lose some of the heat she had.

"What can I do?" she cried. "I know! I will find
other warm coals and together we can warm one
another!" And they did. Together they warmed one
another until they were all burning with enthusiasm
for clean houses. Off to their homes they ran, burning
brightly. And when they needed warming up again,
they just ran back to the pile.

ruined by alcohol and who was unable to conquer it.
They met together, day after day, working on their own
sobriety and formulating the principles that later became the foundation for Alcoholics Anonymous.

These two men, working together in their own private
self-help group, found the help they needed. Today, there
are a million alcoholics in A.A., and millions more have
been helped over the years.

Local Support Groups

Today self-help groups are booming. There are groups
to help gamblers, drug addicts, bald men, widows, ter-
minally ill people, heart attack victims, mastectomy
patients, and many, many others. Some follow the A.A.
Twelve Steps to Sobriety format. Others do not. But all
are alike in that they are needy people, banded together
for mutual aid.

Glen Evans in *The Family Circle Guide to Self-Help*
writes:

Of course there will be those who make significant improvement in their homes and way of life without being a part of a self-help group. However, experience shows us that some will not improve on their own and that those who could improve by struggling alone will be able to improve more consistently and more permanently with support from a group.

Messies Anonymous self-help groups are for women and men who struggle to overcome disorganization in the home. They are extremely important in helping the needy Messie catch the fire of change and keep it. Information on how to start a group and how the twelve steps apply to the problem of messiness is found in the book *Hope for the Hopeless Messie* by Sandra Felton, which is available on www.messies.com.

A word should be said here about the therapy principles of self-help. Not only are we helped directly when we attend but also indirectly when we help other members of the group. As we help others in the group by our participation at group meetings, being available to a partner by phone, or actually assisting one another with organizing the house, we are helped.

An old proverb says,

Help thy brother's boat across and lo!
thine own has reached the shore.

Saint Francis of Assisi wrote in his well-known prayer, "It is in giving that we receive."

A leader of a self-help group in California writes:

My friends (five of them) and I have been trying to support each other using the Messies book. So far so good. We read some chapters aloud and pair up for closets. I can see many changes occurring in me and my house and I am getting a lot of good feedback (and cooperation) from the family.

Listen—if Bill W. and Dr. Bob could do it, so can we. How hard can it be?

On-line Groups

Groups that meet on the Internet have the advantage that they are available every place and any time. They can also be more focused, covering singles, moms, beginners, those down the line in recovery, and other special interests and lifestyles. Messies Anonymous on-line support groups are available (www.messies.com), as are other groups which you can locate with an Internet search.
"You alone can do it, but you can't do it alone."
Check one of the statements below that expresses your feelings:

__Wow, this is great! I want to get involved in a self-help group.
__What! Are you crazy! I can't start a self-help group! I'm already too busy! I'm so disorganized anyway I don't think I could handle it!
__An Internet group sounds good. I'll try that.

However, if I ever did want to think of starting a local group:

1. We could probably meet at _____
2. The day that would be best for me to meet would be _____
3. I could probably find people to come by
   a. asking my friend

217

    b. telling my church friends or club friends.

    c. putting a little notice in the paper. (That's usually free, I think.)

  4. I should probably get the *Hope for the Hopeless Messie* guidebook for twelve-step groups.

But, of course, we all know I could never do that. Still, a group to warm my coals would be helpful . . . Well, maybe I could.

I think I will look up an on-line support group on www.messies.com and see how that works for me. I definitely need to find some kind of additional support and motivation.

Boy, am I glad you found me! I was just beginning to think I was an absolutely hopeless case! My sister bought your book, but she decided I needed it more than she did, so she donated it to a good cause. It was, without a doubt, the best thing ever to enter my house.

About 15 months ago, my husband and I moved into a brand-new, just-built, never-before-lived-in apartment. I thought, "This is great! I get a fresh start. It'll be so easy to keep clean. I'll organize everything as we move in, and it'll be so easy to maintain!" Well, needless to say, my home is in the worst shape it's ever been in.

THANK YOU! THANK YOU, THANK YOU!!

Annette / California

More Reading

Other Books by Sandra Felton

Published by Fleming H. Revell: *The New Messies Manual*—the flagship book for change; *The Messie Motivator; Messie No More; Neat Mom, Messie Kids;* and *When You Live with a Messie.* All of her books have been translated into German; some into Spanish and Chinese.

Available on the website www.messies.com

Why Can't I Get Organized? (on attention deficit disorder)

Time Management for Teachers (on teacher time management)

Organize to Write (on organization for writers)

I've Got to Get Rid of This Stuff (on dejunking excess)

Hope for the Hopeless Messie (on the twelve-step program)

On the Right Brain/Left Brain

Ornstein, Robert, and Richard Thompson. *The Amazing Brain.* Boston: Houghton Mifflin, 1984.

Restak, Richard. *The Brain.* New York: Bantam, 1984.

Zdenek, Marilee. *The Right Brain Experience.* New York: Mc-Graw-Hill, 1983.

On Restoring Order to Your House

Aslett, Don. *Clutter's Last Stand.* Cincinnati: Writer's Digest, 1983.

___. *Do I Dust or Vacuum First?* Cincinnati: Writer's Digest, 1982.

___. *Is There Life after Housework?* Cincinnati: Writer's Digest, 1981.

___. *Not for Packrats Only.* New York: Plume, 1991.

___. *Who Says It's a Woman's Job to Clean?* Cincinnati: Writer's Digest, 1986.

Campbell, Jeff. *Clutter Control: Putting Your Home on a Diet.* New York: Dell, 1992.

Forman, Monte, with the editors of Consumer Reports Books. *How to Clean Practically Everything.* New York: Consumer Reports, 1986.

Rich, Jason. *The Everything Organize Your Home Book.* Avon, MA: Adams Media, 2002.

Roth, Eileen. *Organizing for Dummies.* New York: Hungry Minds, 2001.

Winston, Stephanie. *Getting Organized.* New York: Warner, 1980.

———. *Getting Organized: Storage.* New York: Warner, 1981.

On Finances

Hunt, Mary. *Debt Proof Your Marriage.* Grand Rapids: Revell, 2003.

Monroe, Paula Ann. *Left-Brain Finance for Right-Brain People: A Money Guide for the Creatively Inclined.* Naperville, IL: Sourcebooks, 1996.

Peterson, Jean Ross. *Organize Your Personal Finances: Turn Chaos into Cash.* White Hall, VA.: Betterway Publications, Inc., 1984.

Tyson, Eric. *Personal Finance for Dummies.* New York: Wiley, 2003.

Mail Order Sources

Messies Anonymous at www.messies.com carries my books and other useful organizing products.

Get Organized at www.shopgetorganized.com or 1-800-803-9400. Check out their many "space-saving innovations to unclutter your life."

The Container Store at www.containerstore.com or 1-800-733-3532. They offer many organizing solutions, for any area of the home or office, including closet design, with free personalized planning service in the stores, over the phone, and online.

Lillian Vernon Catalogs at www.lillianvernon.com or 1-800-545-5426. Their household organizing catalog called Neat Ideas emphasizes decorative organizers and tools for every room in the house. Lillian Vernon, 510 South Fulton Avenue, Mount Vernon, NY 10550. Wonderful, inexpensive helps for getting your life in order.

Hold Everything, A Catalogue of Household Ideas from Williams-Sonoma, P.O Box 7456, San Francisco, CA 94120-7456. You never in your life saw so many things that hold things. Great help and inspiration.

I've been meaning to write to you, but—well, you know how it is!! Seriously, next to the Bible, your book has done more to change and improve my life than anything else.

Nina / Connecticut

I was so valiantly attacking a stack of newspapers in my tiny studio apartment, when I scanned an article in a January New York Times (I think it was January, but it could have been an '85 paper). I'm overly qualified for membership, unfortunately.

I've been cleaning my apartment for seven years, with only a handful of days to show that I've ever made any progress. I'm a collector of many things, I'm a rather organized but cluttery person in the office, I call my studio "the closet," I rationalize like crazy, I must be somewhat content living like this although I'm more than ready to change (if possible).

I have what seem to be good reasons for keeping things—many things, but I can't find "a place" for each thing I keep. So tell me, do I qualify?

I have great hopes of making some improvements. I'm finding great humor in the idea of this membership, great redemption that there are others like me, and I will carry my membership card with pride.

Diane / New York

Sandra Felton, The Organizer Lady™, is the author of many books on bringing order and beauty to the home, including the best-selling *The New Messies Manual* and *Messie No More.* She is founder and president of Messies Anonymous, a group for those who seek a new and better way of life. Through her encouragement and information, many have found relief and brought organization and harmony to their lives, homes, and family life. For more information, log on to www.messies.com.

Sandra speaks at women's conferences and is a frequent guest on national radio and TV shows. She lives with her husband in Miami, Florida.